Growing Through Grief

Words from the heart that will help you to find the Gift in grief

ANTHOLOGY

Growing Through Grief:

Words from the heart that will help you to find the GIFT in grief

Copyright © 2025 Linda Ledwidge

No part of this book may be reproduced in any form without written permission from the publisher or author, except as permitted under the **Copyright Act 1968.**

Linda Ledwidge asserts her right to be identified as the primary author of this work under the **Copyright Amendment (Moral Rights) Act 2000.**

Disclaimer: The authors make no representations or warranties regarding any information provided in this book, including treatments, actions, or the application of medication. Readers should seek professional advice where appropriate.

Every effort has been made to obtain the necessary copyright permissions. Any omissions or errors are unintentional and will be corrected in future printings if required.

Book Cover: "Image from Wallpapers.com."

ISBN: 9798319141491

Independently published

Your Authors

DIAMONDS

Anon

Linda Ledwidge

Gail Ledwidge   Jenny Ledwidge

Sue Berry   Lisa Ferris   Glynis German

Stephanie Schulz   Vicki McLeod   Deirdre Maguire

Ayelet Baron   Laura Penn

Amanda J Butler

Valou

ANTHOLOGY

"Grief is the echo of love that has nowhere to go—so it settles in your bones and teaches you to carry it."

Gratitude

AND APPRECIATION FROM LINDA LEDWIDGE

This book was born from my own journey through life and the realisation that I had gone through the *"grief process"* more than once. Along the way, I encountered countless lightbulb moments and failed to recognise the transformations they brought, until 2014, when I had no choice but to face them with full awareness. I thought then that I had nailed it; how wrong I was! 2024 was to bring me another lightbulb moment. Have I nailed it now? Probably not, I hope not because we always have room to grow and BEcome. That is what life is about.

How can I thank every person and appreciate every experience that has helped me grow? That is a momentous task, so I will Keep It Super Simple, as I like to do....

Thank you!

To the authors of this book, you have my utmost admiration and respect. I am in awe of you. Because of you, so many people will find the inspiration to grow through grief and find the *gift*.

You rock!

To you, the reader

Thank you- for being **Y O U!**

Zoot Zoot Zoot

♥ · ♥ · ♥ · ♥ · ♥

Our thanks to the following people for giving me permission to include their work:

Bruce Coville for allowing me to use the quote from his book, Jeremy Thatcher, Dragon Hatcher
Nothing You Love is Lost.
(c) 1991

Sharyn Marsh for allowing me to publish her words from the heart of 11th of January 2024 on her Leave Her Wild Facebook page.

Helen Lapierre for allowing me to publish her poem *'Let Them In,'* her words from the heart that let us know we are not alone.

Becky Hemsley, whose poem *'Glass Balloon'* is from the book *When I Am Gone: Poems for times of loss and grief.*
Wildmark Publishing (February 23, 2023)

For Mum, Dad, & Susan

My pillars,

Always with me

xc

ANTHOLOGY

"You don't 'get over' grief—you grow around it, like tree roots around a stone."

To the Reader

GRIEF IS A UNIVERSAL EXPERIENCE

"Grief is just a five-letter word. Simple, right? *BUT* is it? If so, it's one of the most powerful five-letter words we know. Then again, words have a way of holding immense power, don't they?"

Grief is often associated with the death of a loved one, and while this is one of the most profound experiences of grief, it is far from the only one. Throughout our lives, we encounter many moments of transformation - times when the life we once knew shifts, evolves, or changes direction. These moments can bring deep emotions, uncertainty, and even a sense of loss as we step into something new.

But within grief, there is a gift.

Grief is not just about losing someone or something; it is about change, growth, and the process of discovering who we are becoming. It can arise during major life transitions - **the end of a relationship, a career shift, moving to a new place, evolving identities, or even personal**

growth that requires us to let go of an old version of ourselves. Each of these experiences asks us to navigate the space between what was and what will be, offering us the opportunity to transform.

At its core, grief is not a single emotion but a journey - emotional, physical, and spiritual. It is our natural response to change, bringing with it a mix of feelings such as sadness, uncertainty, anger, hope, and even relief. The depth of our grief reflects the significance of what is shifting in our lives, and while it can be painful, it also holds the potential for something powerful: renewal.

The five stages of grief - **denial, anger, bargaining, depression, and acceptance** - are commonly used to describe this process. However, these stages are not a rigid framework. You may not experience them in order, you may skip some entirely, or you may revisit certain emotions multiple times. **Grief is not a set path;** it is a deeply personal transformation that unfolds in its own way and in its own time.

Many people experience grief before a major change even occurs - perhaps during a period of uncertainty, the slow ending of a chapter, or the realisation that life is shifting in a way they did not expect. Others may only recognise their grief long after a transition has happened when emotions surface unexpectedly. Wherever you are in this process, know that your feelings are valid, and your journey is your own.

This book is not about "moving on" from grief, as if it were something to be left behind. Instead, it is about *growing through grief* - embracing change, learning from it, and discovering the unexpected gift it offers. Grief can be painful, but it is also a teacher. It can reveal what truly matters, deepen our understanding of ourselves, and help us rebuild our lives in a way that honours both our past and our future.

If you are reading this, you are likely in the midst of a transition. Whether your experience of grief is tied to the loss of a loved one, a personal transformation, or an unexpected change in your path, know that you are not alone. This book is here to walk with you - to offer understanding, comfort, and guidance as you navigate this deeply personal journey.

You will never be exactly who you were before this transformation, but that is not something to fear. In time, and in your own way, you will come to see that the change grief brings is not just an ending, but a **gift** - an invitation to grow, to deepen, and to step into the next chapter of your life with wisdom, resilience, and a renewed sense of self.

Whenever you need to... take a breath, take a minute, and take a look around you... You are where you are, and that's OK.

To **YOU**, from all of the people who have contributed to this book,

"We see YOU."

ANTHOLOGY

Beneath the weight, in quiet dark,

Where sorrow pressed a lasting mark,

A spark remained, however small—

A light that didn't fade at all.

No blazing fire, no bursting flame,

Just something soft that grief became.

A gleam, a glow, a fractured shine—

A heart, reshaped, now diamond-fine.

~Linda ~

Contents

The Silence of Grief	XVI
Grief - Myths Exploded	1
Myths About Grief	
Breathe	4
The Deeper the Love - The Deeper the Grief by Sue Berry	5
Leave Her Wild by Sharyn Marsh	9
Growing Through Tears by Glynis German	11
Sorrow	30
Empty Nest by Stephanie Schulz	31
Who Am I?	40

GRIEF, grief, GRIEF by Gail Ledwidge	41
A Grief	48
Growing Through the Love by Jenny Ledwidge	49
Grief Is Tough by Laura Penn	65
Zooties from My Heart to Your Heart	68
My story behind grief Anonymous	69
Grief is just Love with no place to go Jamie Anderson	76
Grief is the process by which we manage to live serenely with the loss of someone or something by Valerie Haesen (Valou)	77
Weep William Shakespeare	80
Transforming Grief into Hope by Deidre MaGuire	81
Grief by Lisa Ferris	93
Let Them In by Helen Lapierre	103

The Gift in Grief Linda Ledwidge	105
Grief Reveals Us by Ayelet Baron	107
YOU are OK	114
Grief and Loss by Amanda J Butler	115
Nothing you love is lost Bruce Coville	156
Signs of Life by Vicki McLeod	157
Life Goes On Linda Ledwidge	167
Navigating Grief Gentle Reminders When You're Hurting	185
Experience Ralph Waldo Emerson	189
About the Authors	191
Grief resources designed for when you or someone you care about needs support in navigating loss	217
Afterword	223
Notes	225

The Silence of Grief

"Sometimes the silence of grief is louder than any goodbye."

Grief – Myths Exploded

MYTHS ABOUT GRIEF

- **Grief follows a set timeline**

Myth: "You should be over it by now."

Truth: Grief has no set expiration date. Everyone grieves in their own time. Some days will feel heavier than others, even years later.

- **You have to be strong**

Myth: "Be strong for your family."

Truth: Being "strong" doesn't mean bottling up emotions. It's okay—and healthy—to cry, talk, rest, or even fall apart for a while.

- **You always move forward**

Myth: "Grief gets better every day."

Truth: Grief isn't linear and it does not heal with time. It can come in waves—better one day, worse the next. Progress doesn't always look like a straight line.

- **Talking about them makes it worse**

Myth: "Don't mention their name—it'll upset them."

Truth: Most grieving people want to talk about their loved one. Sharing memories can be comforting and healing.

- **If you're laughing, you're not grieving properly**

Myth: "You seem fine—you must be over it."

Truth: Crying is not obligatory to grieve. Joy and sorrow can live side by side. Laughing or enjoying life doesn't mean the grief has gone away.

- **In time, the grief will go away**

Myth: "Grief is something you get over."

Truth: Grief is a process, it does not end, it changes. It becomes part of who you are, not something you leave behind.

- **Grief is only about death**

Myth: "You're grieving? Who died?"

Truth: Grief can come from many types of loss—relationships, identity, health, or even dreams for the future.

- **Ignoring the pain will help it go away in time**

Myth: "Time is a great healer"

Truth: Time does not heal a physical trauma, so why would you expect it to heal an emotional trauma? Grief is an emotional trauma, and as with physical trauma, healing is promoted by seeking help and support.

Breathe

"This, too, shall pass."
~ A line from a Middle Eastern fable, Persian most likely~

The Deeper the Love – The Deeper the Grief

by Sue Berry

I have "lost" 4 special people who made a great impact on my life of 73 years.

I stress "lost" because they are NOT lost. They are buried deep within my heart, psyche, body, and soul forever.

Someone once said to me, "You grieve for yourself." At the time, I did not understand, but now I understand that when you KNOW you have given all the love, support, strength, and stamina that you possess, it is natural to feel let down and disappointed in yourself, and you feel "lost" and abandoned.

My grandmother, Jane, passed away peacefully in my arms when I was 16. She was 76 and had been afraid of death all her life.

She was afraid of death, but in her final moments, she glowed. I know she saw someone or something in the corner of the room, and she was happy to go and join them.

It was quite amazing to witness.

I also had the privilege of nursing my mother, Edna, my husband, and then my partner through cancer, both of them for around 6 months. My mother passed away peacefully in the hospital. She was ready to go. Edna was only 73 years old.

My husband, John, died during an operation for bowel cancer in 1992. He was 53. We had only been married for 2 years, but we spent a wonderful 19 years together, the very best years of my life.

5 years after his death, I was struggling to hold myself together and do my job, which was in the public eye. I tried to commit suicide; I took pills with vodka; I slit my wrists, and I even threw myself under a bus—all within 24 hours.

During my time in a mental hospital, I had a vision of my mother and my husband together pushing me away. It wasn't my time; thankfully, I pulled through, but I do remember that terrible and frightening experience so very well.

My partner, Derek, died in a hospital in 2008.

He was 73 and suffering from lung cancer. I have never seen such determination to live; we lived in constant hope and fear. Hope and fear—that's the cycle.

I found that being able to talk openly and frankly about our innermost feelings during this traumatic time helped me enormously during my grief afterward.

Having good friends around me during this time was a tremendous help, as I have no living family.

One of the hardest parts of the grieving process is acceptance. When you've achieved this, you're on your way to peace of mind.

I'm not a religious person, per se. But I do believe in angels. They appear in different forms and situations. I have been amazed by their response!

My biggest trigger during grieving was when I was forced to sell my or our home due to probate taking 3 years and not the 6 months that I was advised by my solicitor. There were 2 countries involved, which made it a bit more difficult. Handing over my keys was heartbreaking, notwithstanding the angst and emotional upset I endured during those 3 awful years. I had hardly any money during the last few months until the contract was signed.

I asked the angels for help, and within half an hour, quite literally, a gentleman came to my door and asked if the item my partner was selling before his death was still for sale; he gave me €300 for the item. I wept and wept and gave my utmost thanks to my angels.

Other triggers for me are music, familiar places, aromas, and seeing couples together in their bubble of happiness. Naturally, all these evoke memories, but I carry my loved ones in my heart and soul every day of my life, and I feel I'm sharing my joy with them. By joy, I mean my mortality. I am grateful that I was able to share the happiest years of my life with 2 loving, kind, genuine, and strong men. They are both beside me, inside me, giving me strength and fortitude to carry on.

I have also had the pleasure of knowing 2 special friends, Helen and Christian, who meant the world to me. Other friends have passed away; however, those friends didn't have the same impact that these 2 wonderful people had on my life.

Dealing with and coping with death in grief is one of the hardest situations we will deal with in our lifetime. How we deal with this—grief is like laughter. It has to come out; otherwise, it's detrimental to our health, mental state, and well-being.

We could find a quiet place and scream, drink alcohol, rant, rave, and cry from our boots. I have done this OR dress your best, go for a walk, meet people who understand. There is an old adage, "Time is a great healer," and it's very true; it does take time.

We learn to live with our grief and feel truly thankful for what we have. Our loved ones would not want us to fall apart, for sure!

I sincerely hope this helps someone who is struggling.

There is a light at the end of this tunnel called the grieving process.

Leave Her Wild

by Sharyn Marsh

Australian writer, Empath, widow, and Free spirit, Sharyn wrote this on the 11th of January 2024

I recently read a quote that said:

> "They were here, and it mattered. You are here, and it matters."

It stopped me in my tracks. When we lose someone so significant in our lives, a part of us dies with them.

In the almost 5 years since my loss, without realising it, I have placed no importance on my existence. In my opinion, I didn't matter, not anymore. My loss and my grief have overshadowed my own existence. Life has been robotic since then, going through the motions yet not really placing any importance on my place here on Earth. I have felt invisible, useless, and depressed beyond anything I've ever experienced before.

Life lost its meaning when he died.

Coming across this quote this week has reminded me that, in fact, I do matter.

I am still here. He was here, and he mattered. I am here, and I matter.

Moving forward, I think the best way to honour him and the beautiful life he led is to re-establish my place here. To live a life that matters. To remember who I was before losing him. To continue to walk through this life with grace and love in my heart. Just like I did before.

He is missing from the earth now and from so many people's lives, but he will never be missing from our hearts. I tuck him away in my heart for safekeeping and will move forward with the belief that I still matter.

♡

Growing Through Tears

by Glynis German

Introduction

> *"You are not just a drop in the ocean, you are the mighty ocean in the drop."*
>
> — Rumi

I don't claim to be an expert on anything, least of all grief. The reason I say this is because I am learning about grief all the time! What I do know, however, is that grief has a way of unravelling and keeping to its own timetable. There's nothing that you or I can do to move grief along. Grief is there, and once accepted, it can be a great lesson for us all.

The Oxford English Dictionary defines grief as mental pain, distress, or intense sorrow, especially caused by someone's death. Note that word "especially," as I want to show you that grief is not necessarily restricted to the death of a loved one. It is important that we recognise when and where grief can happen and give ourselves permission to feel and process it.

Grief is what happens when loss is experienced, most commonly as a response to losing someone or something. Grief is what we think of when a death occurs, yet grief is also a response in other instances, such as divorce, losing a limb or body part, being made redundant or retiring, having to suddenly leave one's home and country, and even having beliefs and ideas challenged.

On speaking with yet another young adult "child," I realised they were grieving the loss of their relationship with their parent. The parent is very much alive and well, but the relationship has been complicated by the parent's new partner, thus impacting the relationship between parent and child.

This young person's anger covers up a lot of the hurt they are feeling. Hurt at not being able to have time alone with their parent. They are sad that their parent no longer spends as much time with them. As they see their parent immerse themselves in the new relationship, making plans that do not include them, often appearing to exclude them, this young adult is hurting.

By providing a listening ear, I have been able to allow this young person to get in touch with their feelings. Those negative thoughts, present and insistent, travelling at great speed through the mind and bringing with them uncomfortable feelings, were allowed to show up and were then able to be transformed through time, space, and understanding.

There are those who are experiencing what is termed "anticipatory grief." It is often those who are caring for a loved one, someone who is terminally ill or elderly, and death is looming on the horizon. Fears around identity (soon they will become an orphan, widow, widower, or vilomah[1]), worries over financial security, and even wondering what their future purpose will be are very real for the carer.

In these instances, I remind the carer to access any helpful resources and to be in the present moment and just be with their loved one—physically, emotionally, mentally, and spiritually. It is always helpful to recognise when and where one needs help, rest, and comfort to be able to continue with their journey.

I try to remember the advice when flying: to put on our own oxygen mask first before helping others. My oxygen mask is on through ongoing study and learning around death and dying, and through the experiences afforded me by being able to support others at their most vulnerable.

PROPOSAL

"The quieter you become, the more you are able to hear."
Rumi

In this chapter, I want to talk to you about the grieving process from my point of view. I shall share from my personal experience of having lived through moments of learning from some intense grieving.

My interpretation of grief that I wish to share is because I have grown through the many lessons grief has taught me. I see grief as an opportunity for personal growth, bringing with it the invitation to transform feelings and find peace.

I will share one of my own biggest grieving experiences, with its accompanying mental pain and distress, that of my divorce, and how many of my lifelong beliefs and opinions were challenged through that experience.

I believe that by sharing what I learned and how I began to understand my feelings it may help others who are struggling with their own grief. I am still learning that grief is ongoing and a process that takes time, along with my openness and willingness to better understand myself.

I have some goals and ambitions with wanting to understand grief. I want to feel more clearly and completely and be able to communicate my feelings rather than suppress them. Surely, with more understanding about feelings, one can hope for a happier experience in life? That's one task I am willing to make time for.

Grief, somewhat annoyingly, has a habit of lying dormant and can take one by surprise by coming through at the least expected moment. To feel or not to feel, this is a question that I enjoy asking myself. Grief is there to teach us and allow us to grow, and it is a process, one that I encourage others to make the space for and be open to.

One of the biggest challenges in our society is understanding feelings. We have become so accomplished at suppressing our feelings, and I especially have maintained a lot of distance from the more unpleasant feelings that have come up for me over the decades of my life.

Now, in my seventh decade, I am willing to go deep and invite patience, gentle acceptance, and compassionate self-care to be my guides. This is a message I often share with families who have said their final goodbye to a loved one and are about to embark on a journey without the physical presence of said loved one.

The journey that accompanies grieving will be filled with opportunities. Sometimes intense and painful, maybe exhausting and debilitating. Hopefully, the journey will bring understanding; that will be up to the traveller.

Perhaps I should tell of my own journey, which began in disbelief and hurt, and which is still taking me to understanding, acceptance, and love. But first, a bit about where I came from.

PERSONAL EXPERIENCE: Upbringing, early years

"What strikes the oyster shell does not damage the pearl."
                                                        Rumi

I was blessed with loving parents and a large and generally happy family. I had a 1960s upbringing, coming from one small island in the Caribbean—Jamaica—to a bigger island in the North Atlantic—Britain.

We came over on a banana boat, the only passengers sailing with that precious freight and bound for a new life. My parents were open to exploring the possibilities ahead, and the air was positive.

We spent the first months living with my maternal grandmother, who had her home on the outskirts of London. We joined her and my step-grandfather while my parents looked for work and a new home for us, their five children.

An incident happened when I had newly arrived in England, just 5 years old, and also new at the local primary school, which was already halfway through the school year. It was this incident that followed me through life, suppressed but present, and I later learned how grief lies dormant, waiting to teach us what we need to learn when we are ready to do so.

This experience of discomfort and confusion led me to become accomplished at suppressing my feelings. I was hurt because of racist name-calling directed at me, which was happening at my new school, being targeted by a couple of boys out of sight of any teachers.

Whilst I felt hurt by the boys' behaviour, I was curious to understand the language they used. What did nig-nog actually mean? My dear, kind, inspiring, and intelligent parents suggested I feel sorry for those boys. Intellectually, yes, I still feel sorry for those trapped in ignorance.

There was a reluctant growing up and closing down experienced with this particular incident. I was no longer an excitable and curious girl child; something had been lost in the confusion of bad behaviour being directed at my person. Being told to feel sorry for those boys shut me down from expressing any uncomfortable feelings for the many decades of my life that were to come.

What suppressing my confusion and hurt did was to close down my self-communication skills and, thus, my ability to understand and accept any feelings that were uncomfortable. Especially uncomfortable from then on were situations that involved me being seen as a white woman rather than the proud woman of mixed heritage I am and having to listen in on racist conversations, the initiators of which assumed I was one of them.

As I look back at the five-year-old mini me, I recognise how deep those wounds went, which took decades to first understand and then to accept. I am still learning to find my voice, so was it a surprise later to have to learn the lessons when my marriage went south? Maybe not.

Shock and disbelief—marriage falls apart

> *"Look for the answer inside your question."*
>
> Rumi

I had been brought up with my beliefs set in stone: marriage was for life; being good was the only way to be, and a polite nature was expected of me. I had also innocently and somewhat ignorantly believed that there was only one model for my womanhood—marriage and children.

Thus, it was devastating to have all my preconceived ideas on what marriage should be challenged by lies and deceit. My journey of self-discovery began, and how grateful I am for the pain, the hurt, the tears, and the eventual emotional and spiritual growth.

The year was 2007, and my partner and I split up after 14 years and two children together. My parents made it to a month off 60 years when my father died, which made it easy to always believe that marriage was for life. *Why would I think any differently?*

It wasn't an easy transition to first separate and then to definitively go our separate ways. I laugh now at how I railed and shook my fists at the windmills; a female *Doña Quijote*, furious at the unfairness of it all. My partner had fallen in love with someone else.

Suddenly we were no more, and I started to feel… rage and disbelief primarily and a lot of tears. I was all cried out for a long time after, years in fact, and it is only recently that I have begun to cry again. At that time, I knew I would have to forgive… one day. This journey of forgiveness had to begin with forgiving myself.

I adopted this willingness to forgive, as I was fortunate to recognise that my part in the breakup had to be owned by me and only me. Starting with my own forgiveness was not easy and was, in fact, painful, uncomfortable, and, at times, even excruciating as I recognised my own bad behaviours.

In hindsight, it's funny how I had long dreamed of having my own space, one where I would be living next door to hubby and kids. Sadly, this model of family in the western world seems to exist only when the family splits up, and it's certainly how we live now—me in my home and the ex, down the road with the kids coming and going still.

However, the pain I felt when we separated was the grief I was experiencing as I grappled with my part in the loss. If only I had been different, softer, slimmer, more interesting, less afraid, speaking up, or standing up for what I wanted and needed. If only… The list was long, and I was devastated as I realised that I only had myself to consider, as I had shut myself out of my marriage.

It came down to me and me alone. The habit of suppressing my feelings, the habit of not speaking up, had allowed me to descend into the part of me that was more comfortable with a migraine taking me out of the picture rather than expressing what I was feeling. Interestingly, after 30 years of suffering from migraines, I no longer have them, but that's another story!

It has been a slow journey and is luckily ongoing as I accept the imperfections that invite me to stop and decide—*do I want this or that? Is any of it necessary for me to hold on to?* That's the beauty of grief; it will challenge us to reconsider beliefs set in stone and invite us to be open to a different meaning in life. And how I've grown in the years since.

My relationship with my ex is healthy, and our sons are beautiful and kind young men who enjoy our company whenever we get together. We are capable of arguing, but we spend more time being able to make plans that include our children, such as eating together or spending special holidays together.

What I learned about myself since that devastating moment when he told me *"I love you, but I am not in love with you"* (whatever that was supposed to mean) is that losing an idea, an experience, or a daily or regular relationship hurts.

However, hurt can be transformed, but only when I put the work in. I felt awful for years. Awful, in that I didn't trust myself or others, which meant there were quite a few changes to relationships that had made sense when I was with my ex. A lot of those types of relationships finished, and I grieved some more for a while.

Eventually, I developed strength in adopting a more positive understanding towards detachment from possessing fixed ideas. I learned to be open to things changing if they had to, and although I have to know where I am going and what I am meant to be doing, I am more and more accepting of any changes, especially when I grow.

Whilst I have now been single for longer than I was in my relationship—it's now 17 years—I occasionally mourn for something so straightforward as an accepted norm, such as marriage, having a partner, or living with someone. Then I stop and think some more and realise how truly fortunate and blessed I am to have all this time for myself and for working on improving this model.

Plus, I have learned what will be, will be, and you never know!

ALL AROUND US—Expressions of Grief

> *"If everything around seems dark, look again, you may be the light."*
>
> Rumi

Difficulties sleeping, hours and hours spent wide awake, the mind racing, sadness and rage mixed in with risky behaviour; not always able to continue to be a kind person to others. All of these behaviours, plus not looking after oneself properly, maybe choosing to work more so as not to feel or think or face what is happening, are all to be expected.

These are indicators of grieving, along with disbelief, crying, being hard on oneself, forgetfulness or foggy minds, disconnection, health issues, and more.

Whilst there are some obvious signs of behaviour in the grieving process, there are different types of grieving too. Traumatic, prolonged, complicated, anticipatory, chronic, delayed, collective, and even disenfranchised grief are just some of the different types of reactions to certain situations.

When a friend's husband died suddenly, it seemed her world had fallen apart some more, when months later, and in the supermarket, they didn't have the bread she normally bought. There and then, she burst into tears and was inconsolable, raging about the bread whilst mourning for her husband. Looking back now, she can laugh at the experience, but that's an example of how grief can catch you unawares.

An acquaintance had concerns for their mother's well-being amid threats of suicide, especially as their relationship was not a positive one. When I probed and questioned the mother's history, especially wishing to know in what year she was born, I wasn't surprised to see so much suffering.

Considering the context of where their mother had grown up (a war-torn community, daily acts of violence, much stress, and tension), they were able to appreciate that this was, amongst other issues, some deep and unresolved grief. By understanding their mother and being mindful of their own experiences of grieving, they were able to do the work necessary for transformation and eventually even improve their relationship.

ONGOING LEARNING

> *"When the light returns to its source, it takes nothing of what it has illuminated."*
>
> Rumi

I am a witness to a lot of emotions in my work, supporting people and holding space. I have seen and thus learned that silence is truly golden; silence that hears, that allows, that invites, that brings comfort. And how silence can heal.

In my work as a facilitator of Death Cafe™ meetups—encounters where one is invited to consider what death means to them—I have seen magic happen. The magic I have witnessed has been the holding of space for those who are deeply immersed in their grief.

I discovered the global Death Cafe™ movement in 2015, just when I had decided that I wanted to offer more support at the end of life. I added funeral training to my celebrant work and happened upon a blog written by a Swede living in London who'd attended her first Death Cafe™.

I was fascinated! A Death Cafe™ was an event where tea, cake, and death were on the menu! Reading more, I was hooked and knew I had to attend one. Searching on the internet, I discovered one happening in Asturias, only a flight away and on the mainland from where I live in Spain!

Frustrated by the discovery yet eager to attend a Death Cafe™, I rang Jon Underwood, the founder of the movement, and asked him if there was a Death Cafe™ in Mallorca. He said yes, and I was ecstatic! Where? I asked. Wherever you want it to be was his response, and thus the Death Cafe™ came to Mallorca in December 2015.

People wonder what a Death Cafe™ is, and quite simply, it is a group of people, relative strangers, who attend for many different reasons. Some are driven by curiosity to understand more about the one guarantee. Some are there because they are caring for a loved one who is either elderly or ill, and they have questions, worries, or doubts. Sometimes, those who are in the deepest pain of grief show up, although a Death Cafe™ is not considered a therapy group.

However, I have seen how holding space for others who are in pain and allowing them space to feel and maybe talk brings out the best in humans. Some Death Cafés™ have had participants on the edge of their chairs, desperate to allow the one in deep grief to know they are with them at that precise moment.

These magical moments have taught me that whilst there is nothing we can do to take away someone's grief, there is the most incredible gift we can make by just being present to their pain.

Silence is golden was one of those many expressions I grew up hearing yet not really understanding. In my work as a celebrant, end-of-life doula, and Death Café™ facilitator, I experience the rewards when we allow silence to just be.

It has taken me time and practice to get comfortable with silence. Having a regular practice of yoga and meditation or walking alone in nature has helped. Officiating celebration of life ceremonies has also shown me how effective moments of silence can be.

I always ponder how words become of little importance when one is in the dying process. I have seen that when love shows up in terms of support, accompaniment, understanding, or just being with a loved one, there is so much that can be said without words.

HEALING POWERS OF CEREMONY

> *"Look inside yourself; everything that you want, you already are."*
>
> Rumi

In a world that markets a quick fix for most pain, these can instead suppress feelings rather than allowing them space to manifest and perhaps to transform. Whilst the pain may be managed with distraction or denial or sometimes even medication, it doesn't just magically go away or disappear, never to appear again.

Seeing how others react in funerals with the release of suppressed emotions allows me to realise how much healing happens within the ceremony. It's often a surprise to me to see the acquaintances who attend a funeral show the emotions they show.

Those feelings may not necessarily be related to the death of the person whose funeral they are attending. Has grief lain dormant or has it been suppressed? What brings me joy is seeing the responses to the ceremony and a sense of calm descend over the mourners, as I witnessed with an adult child who came on holiday to where I live. Their partner had the very wise idea that this could be the perfect time and place to have a ceremony for the parent who had died the previous year.

The circumstances around the death and subsequent funeral had brought a set of challenges that meant that the funeral did not bring the calm and peace that the adult child had hoped and longed for. The year was 2020, and only six were allowed to attend the funeral, as long as they remained physically distant from each other.

On holiday they came, with partner and young children, having previously confirmed me for the ceremony. They commented that after our very first online conversation, in which I needed to get to know their parent, they were surprised to be feeling relieved after talking about their experience of the previous year.

The day came for the ceremony, and the location was one they chose in the days after arriving at their hotel, when the adult child had chosen to go off walking on their own to scout out the perfect place. These were suggestions I had made, knowing that feeling empowered to make these types of decisions would help with the grieving process.

Much joy was experienced, along with inevitable tears. Sadness was felt, relief too, and with the ceremony, the family was able to feel that the chapter was closed, and they could now move forward with fond and loving memories of a life lived.

My intention with any ceremony is to invite families to participate as much as they want and feel able to do so. Whilst many imagine that they won't be able to speak at the funeral, believing that tears will hold them back, I have yet to find a family member who does not finish what they set out to say on the day of a funeral.

Empowering families is to hold space for them and to hear them, both in what is said and in what can often be unsaid. Clarity and empathy with a touch of humour are some of the tools I need for this work. Flexibility, being open, and never being in a hurry (funerals are often held 36 hours from death in Spain) allow family members to feel respected and heard. They become present by the end of the final goodbye.

Getting to know a loved one from family members and then writing about them before saying a final goodbye should be a positive experience. From meeting with the family and spending time talking about their loved one, looking at photos, trinkets, mementos, or even trophies and awards can bring peace and calm.

Witnessing the families at the beginning of the meeting and saying goodbye to them a few hours later is humbling. They have allowed a relative stranger into their lives who has seen them at their most vulnerable.

To then see them a few days later, at the funeral, going through all the emotions that appear and then seeing them leave after the ceremony, that leaves me in awe at the capacity of humans to find strength even when they believe they don't have any.

RESOLUTION—Wrapping up my thoughts

> *"It's your road, and yours alone. Others may walk it with you, but no one can walk it for you."*
>
> Rumi

The journey of life is unique and singular. Life experiences will include triumphs and challenges, losses and gains. Grief will join us at times, and we can invite grief to be our friend instead of rejecting or suppressing the gifts grief brings. Consider grief as the best friend who tells you what you need to know in order to grow, the one who is always there for you.

And just as death, along with any type of loss, can show up as an unexpected and unwanted surprise, the way we greet and receive the experience will be an opportunity. The choice to use this opportunity for personal growth is unique to each one of us, and the rewards that accompany choosing to grieve can be plentiful.

As I said at the beginning of this chapter, I am not an expert on grief. I am a human being who has lived and who has been offered many types of life experiences. Some have been painful and others splendidly joyful. I have taken them all as gifts for my personal and spiritual growth, as I believe I was born to be happy.

My life journey has gifted me opportunity, blessings, and learning, and I have taken them all in gratitude and love. My faith in something bigger than me has kept me going and allowed me to find strength when I felt weak.

I don't have answers for people who are in the depths of their mourning. I only know that there is light ahead, just as the day becomes night, which in turn becomes day again. I know that the future will be better than today.

Yet the future depends on how I handle today and the choices I make. There will be good days and bad days. Perhaps it will help to count your blessings on the good days and remind yourself of them on the bad days.

As Rumi said, "When will you begin that long journey into yourself?"

Rumi also said, "Try something different. Surrender."

Why not surrender to your feelings and also to yourself, a self that truly feels… loss, the state of overwhelm and sadness? And then surrender yourself to the idea that this, too, will change.

Five-year-old mini me may have been shut down temporarily, but the experience allowed her to feel how words and actions can impact others. Hopefully, the words above will have allowed you, the reader, to learn to be gentle on yourself in your grieving and be open to the magic that grieving can gift.

From that small island in the Caribbean to now another small island in the Mediterranean, I reflect on all that I have done in these seven decades. It has led me to appreciate that I am truly blessed, as I am still learning about life. I will continue this learning with thanks to all those people and experiences who contributed, as without their participation, I would not be the woman I am today.

The lessons I have learned include the realisation that, as I came in alone, I will leave here alone; there were people waiting for my arrival here just as there will be those waiting for my arrival elsewhere. Every cloud does have a silver lining, and the sun is always there; whether I see it today, tomorrow, or next week, it will be shining somewhere in the world.

1. a parent who has lost a child. The word is Sanskrit and means *against the natural order.*

Sorrow

"Give sorrow words; the grief that does not speak knits up the over-wrought heart and bids it break."
~William Shakespeare, Macbeth~

Empty Nest

by Stephanie Schulz

I had a plan.

A good one at that. I used to brag to people that I had been very smart when it came to planning our family because my two daughters had been born with an age difference of nine years.

> "This way, I will never have to suffer from empty nest syndrome! When Valentina is nineteen and leaves for university, Martina will be about ready to start her family, and there will be grandkids very soon, so all will be perfect."

Then, when Valentina was about to turn seventeen, Sid, her Belgian boyfriend, asked her if she would consider coming with him to live in Belgium, as he was going to start university in Antwerp that same year in September. I still remember the excitement on her face when she told me and, of course, asked for my opinion. And what was I supposed to do? The COVID-19 pandemic had struck the world only a bit over a year before, turning things completely upside down. Everything had changed, and especially my view of how the world was supposed to go had changed.

I had and still have a strong feeling that we should always choose adventure before dullness and happiness before "how things have always been done.".

We live in Mallorca, Spain, and the Spanish have a lovely saying:

> "¡Qué me quiten lo bailao!" which vaguely translates to "They cannot take away the dances I have already danced".

I 100% live by that saying, and I hope and know that I have taught my daughters the same, especially after the world stood still for months during 2020.

So, I spoke to the kids' Dad, my ex-husband, and we found a way for Valentina to continue her school studies in Antwerp and graduate there. We both agreed that this would be a great opportunity for her to explore the world and become more independent two years before she was supposed to. And what could possibly go wrong? Worst-case scenario, she would come back home.

"Aren't you going to feel alone now that Valentina is moving away to Belgium?"—this was what concerned friends kept asking me, as her departure date approached. My answer invariably was always the same. "Me? Nope! Why would I? I am not the Mum who gets her satisfaction *out of washing my kid's clothes to perfection and preparing healthy, home-cooked meals. I don't depend on smothering my kids to bits. I find my fulfilment in my work, my writing, and my projects. I am a creative Mum, and I love my kids; of course, I do, but I am also happy when I don't need to cook every day and look after someone else's needs all the time. This way, I will be able to write a lot more and fully explore my art!"* Yep. That's what I said, and that is also what I was fully convinced of...in April.

The lengthiness of that speech could have been an indicator of what was about to happen, but I ignored it, of course. Also, I thought that I was prepared because Martina had moved out about six years earlier. (Turns out, you can be sad about the same situation twice).

But the closer August came, and with August the day of Valentina's departure to a different country for at least two years, the more I started feeling—and ignoring—a certain underlying sensation that didn't quite agree with the cool Mum I was displaying on the outside.

I like to be prepared for things, and so I thought with the right strategy, all would be very easy and under control. I started watching sad movies the week before Valentina's departure because I felt if only I could get it out of my system, I would be fine. I watched each and every episode of all the Netflix shows that featured adult kids leaving for college, playing the moment of goodbye on repeat for several days. I cried on repeat, too, and so I felt prepared for the day. I used to believe that I knew myself very well, and that I was always aware of my feelings (and that is usually true!)

The flight from Mallorca to Belgium was supposed to leave at 7:15 in the morning, meaning that we had to get up and go to the airport at around 4 o'clock.

Valentina was, of course, excited, but we both cried a bit when we said goodbye before she entered the security area. I waved and waved until my youngest daughter had disappeared in the duty-free section of the airport. I walked to my ex-husband's car and cried a bit more, but I didn't want to show too many feelings in front of him. Anyway, early flights should not be used for emotional departures.

He dropped me off at my place, and I walked up the four flights of stairs, tired. I opened the door of my apartment. It was empty, of course, and it felt so utterly weird. I sat down on my couch, and I felt empty, too. It was 6 in the morning, not a good time to be a toughie. I have never been a morning person, and taking my kid to the airport at 4 am was not a good idea if I wanted to keep it together. So, there I sat, wanting to cry it out, because I felt that was what I was supposed to do. But for some reason, I couldn't.

So, what then? I made myself a cup of coffee, and while I stood on the terrace, listening to how the city of Palma de Mallorca was slowly waking up, I also listened inside myself. Weirdly, and for the first time in my life, there was nothing there. Not good, not bad. Just nothing. Only a heavy something I was not completely able to decipher.

Ok, I thought, maybe I am just tired. I should just take a nap and go back to sleep. And actually, it felt a bit like a hangover, so I went back to bed with my coffee mug. I scrolled around a bit on my phone to entertain my brain, but nothing could catch my attention for long. After a while, I fell asleep.

Around lunchtime, I had an appointment at the town hall; I had to get my public transport card renewed, so I went there, still exhausted, and stood in line for what felt like an eternity. Finally, I got everything done; I exchanged a couple of jokes with the lady behind the counter and got my new card. Then I made a mistake. Turns out that Modern Family, The Middle, and Gilmore Girls could not prepare me for what was coming next. I decided to buy myself a protection cover for my shiny, new bus card because that was, of course, an essential thing to do the day my daughter moved away to another country.

I walked over to what we call a Chinese store here in Mallorca. It was one of those typical businesses where one can buy everything from paperclips to toys and hardware like tools, curtains, etc.

I was standing in front of a display of different plastic covers, trying to decide which one was the best to protect the bus card I barely ever use. Next to me in the aisle, there was a Mum with her very young, very blonde daughter, maybe four or five years old. The kid reminded me a lot of Valentina and Martina when they were little. They were choosing a puzzle of some sort, and the girl was excited about the new toy she got to choose to take home. I could tell that it was a hard choice between that *"Frozen"* puzzle and another one that featured *"Tinkerbell,"* and while I was struggling with my own life-changing decision, I listened to the conversation between the two of them. And then, out of the blue, it hit me—that would never be me again. My kids still needed me, sure, someday I would probably be a grandmother, and probably, I would even take my grandkids out to fascinating shopping plans, but at that moment I couldn't care less.

At that moment, I realised that I would never be that Mum again. I threw the plastic cover on the shelf; I felt that I had to leave that place immediately. I ran out of the store, stumbled out on the street, and started sobbing so hard that people turned around and stared at me. I couldn't believe myself. I ran to my car, sat inside, and cried and cried and cried. After a while, I started feeling better, slightly relieved by the tears, and I managed to walk to the machine, pay for the parking, and drive myself home. On the way, I called Martina; I was in desperate need of a hug, even if it was only over the phone. It helped, and somehow things started to look up a little.

The next few days were hard; I tried to keep myself busy, but my brain was foggy, and it was hard to focus on anything. I spent my time watching TV. Googling support chats for empty nest syndrome didn't feel helpful, as I couldn't identify with any of the people in those chats. Nothing bad about them; everyone is entitled to their feelings, but nothing that was said in those chats seemed to be especially helpful for me or relate to my situation.

Being a very positive person, I have never liked to feel weak or complain. And I think that was the worst part of the whole situation: I hadn't seen it coming at all and did not know how to deal with it. I was frustrated with myself; all I wanted was to stop being this sad, whiny, poor-me creature I deeply disliked.

At some point, I realised that what I felt was a weird form of grief. That didn't make it better, as I felt ridiculous for those feelings and ungrateful. The biggest fear of a mother is not that her children will leave the house someday. That is the natural thing to happen and for many people something to look forward to. Feeling grief because my daughter had moved almost two thousand km away is by far not comparable to what parents feel who have lost a child. I did not feel entitled to those feelings. My biggest issue with all of this was myself. Part of me had decided for a while that the whole empty nest thing was stupid and that there was no point in making a drama out of missing my daughter.

Brilliant idea, I know.

My feelings didn't only come from missing my daughter. I was not alone; I had my older daughter, Martina, all this time, who lives with her boyfriend very close to me and was a great help through all of this, especially as she was also missing her sister, and we could share our feelings. But it was not that. I was grieving about the happy times when the kids were little, a time that would never come back in the same way, because that younger version of me was gone, too. In a way, I was probably also grieving for the family that was not there anymore and for the marriage that had ended eight years ago and that I had been too busy to mourn when we split up.

I am not one to cry and suffer. I am one to find a plan, a strategy. And so I did. I signed up for the gym again. I started going out at least three times a week. I worked more than ever. I networked so hard that I think no one on the island knows more people than I do. And I started scheduling flights to Belgium for me and from Belgium to Mallorca for Valentina.

Christmas came, and things became a bit easier. I still felt brain foggy, and I still wasn't 100% myself, but I had successfully managed to keep myself busy enough to not notice how I was feeling inside.

And then, about 6 months after Valentina had moved out, something crucial happened. I will always remember that afternoon when I met up with my friend Andrea for a coffee.

We sat in that cute little cafe by the sea, and she asked me how I was doing. I adjusted my sunglasses, took a sip from my rosé (who says coffee, also says wine, don't judge me), and said, *"Great! The whole empty nest thing is finally behind me, I think. I feel so much better!"*

Andrea looked at me, doubtful, and said, *"Really? Took me three years, and I am still not okay with our son going away to university."*

That moment was so incredibly eye-opening to me. Not only that, Andrea, who is one of the tougher ladies in my friends' group, was going through the same thing, but she was also absolutely fine with it and had learnt to embrace it. That was the only way to do it, as with any emotion or state of mind. Feel it, hate it if you wish, but then accept those emotions and embrace them.

The stages of grief are well known, and it is not in any way different when it comes to empty nest syndrome.

Acceptance is key, and the relief that comes with it is unmeasurable, at least in my case. When my friend Andrea said that sentence, a tonne of weight fell off my soul. It was ok to feel the way I felt. I was entitled to my feelings. That night I cried again and on the next day and a couple of times after that. Slowly, I started noticing the days it felt worse but also the days that felt lighter. I realised that I had gone through a weird form of depression, and by acknowledging that, I allowed myself to heal.

Now, two years have gone by, and Valentina is probably going to spend her first year of university in Mallorca, so I will have her at home for some time, which is nice. But I have made my peace with the fact that I am older now, that a new stage of life has started, and that this new phase is actually very exciting. Of course, sometimes I still look back with a smile to the times when the kids were younger, and I used to pick them up from school. But it is nice now to have my girls as friends who like spending time with me. I feel like those last two years have made me realise a lot about myself, and I am still learning.

Do I have any amazing advice for whoever is going through this situation?

Probably not, as there is no magical recipe that works for everyone. But acceptance is a big part of it, and so is the will to cut oneself some slack. We are allowed to feel sad about whatever makes us feel sad. Just sit through it a bit, and let the pain be there for a while. It is not about suffering on purpose, but the strategy of numbing my feelings with too many social activities, travel, and work was definitely not a good idea for me.

But who knows? It might be different for you.

One thing I know for sure is that the dances I have already danced, meaning the wonderful times I had when my kids were little, are never going to be taken away from me, and there are a lot more dances yet to come!

Who Am I?

"Who in the world am I? Ah, that's the great puzzle."
~Lewis Carroll , Alice in Wonderland~

GRIEF, grief, GRIEF

by Gail Ledwidge

It was never linear; sometimes it was quiet, and sometimes it was loud. Some days I wanted to scream at the world to stop; how could it all just keep going on?

My life had changed so much. Sometimes I wanted to hide away, get off this revolving world that just kept going, but it didn't and doesn't work like that.

Life goes on, and that used to anger me.

Life goes on!

Does it?

Not for me, it didn't.

Except it did, just not in the manner it used to.

My first real experience, 1998, at 20 years old, 7 and 1/2 months pregnant, living with a violent partner, already questioning my life choices; how would I manage a baby in amongst the already chaos?

Cue tailspin, cue depression, cue feeling the lowest I've ever been, because the person that I thought was going to guide me and help me the way she had done throughout my life suddenly and unexpectedly died at age 42.

My Mum, my guidance, my support, my reassurance, and my giver of love was cruelly ripped away.

My parents went on holiday to Egypt for 2 weeks, and they flew home late at night. My Mum phoned to check in on me, and I was excited to tell her how I had gone from having hardly any bump, and in 2 weeks it had really popped; I was going to go down and see them, but it was after 10 pm, so we said we would see each other in the morning.

How wrong we were.

The next morning at approximately 6 am, I received a hysterical call from my Dad; he and my brother were awaiting an ambulance. The effects of what happened to her were similar to having a heart attack; nothing could be done. It had been pancreatitis.

Possibly, for months after it, I likely had a form of PTSD. A few times whilst out driving, if an ambulance was behind me in the car and I couldn't get out of the way quick enough, or what I deemed to be quick enough, I used to pull over in the car once it passed, and I'd sob, paranoid I was the cause of someone else dying.

Twenty-five years on, I'm writing this, and 25 years on, have I truly ever dealt with it?

When my mother died, I had 8 weeks that I couldn't go down the "have a drink to blot it out route."

I had 8 weeks to prepare to be a mother while burying my own. 8 weeks to organise for a life to leave this world, but the same 8 weeks to prepare for a life to enter the same one.

There was also a business to run. If I thought I was going to grieve, take my time to heal, and prepare for my baby, I was mistaken. My father entirely lost his grip on reality; the guidance he had in his life was gone, and he didn't know how to survive.

On reflection, I often wonder, do women cope better? Are we predisposed to pick up the pieces? To plate spin and multitask and just keep going.

My mother and father owned a business; they were responsible for other people's livelihoods too. The business had to be run.

However, my father became paralysed with grief; he couldn't function, and he turned to drink.

My brother also couldn't step in; I was involved in the business, but my brother wasn't; he was only 18. He was also totally traumatised by trying to resuscitate my mother and it not working, whilst my father rocked back and forth in the corner of my parent's bedroom, unable to assist in pure panic.

It left me; I picked myself up and got on with it.

I ran the business; I ran my house, and I ran my parent's house, and in between times, I had my first baby. I feel I may have *'got off the tiniest bit lighter'* than my brother; he was still in my parent's home, where it all happened; he was just a teenager, now not only dealing with a mother who has died but also failing to save her. *(He would NEVER have been able to; I only hope he knows this.)*

I can now say I probably ran from the grief too; I was too busy to be upset, and I was too distracted to allow myself time. I think I closed myself off; I didn't allow myself the pain, the acceptance, the change.

It hurt; it hurt a damn lot, but I couldn't and wouldn't allow myself to fall apart, to grieve. I mentally and physically never allowed myself.

Even now, I'm unsure of how to 'tell the story' of my grief. I hid from it; I likely still do.

You only get one mother: I feel I lost her at one of the pivotal times in my life. There was the shock that gave way to anger, followed by disappointment, sadness, and regret. It left lots of questions that burled about in my busy brain.

I wish I could say I did XYZ, and that made it better; the truth be known, I've still no idea how I got through it. One foot in front of the other and to keep breathing must have been enough on some days.

If I thought that I had almost gotten through that, then life was going to test me again.

My second experience of real grief, 2009-2011, now with 2 children and a new partner (husband 2001) and fairly settled with what life can throw at you.

My father was diagnosed with bladder cancer. We watched him fight very gracefully; you would never have known he was unwell.

In 2011, we spent Christmas in the hospital praying (I'm not religious, but when you have no hope, you have nothing). I prayed very selfishly that my Dad didn't die on one of the 'big' days, Christmas Eve, Christmas Day, or Boxing Day, as I knew they would have never been the same; how could I go on again for my children if every year it was an anniversary of being so sad?

He must have listened, as he waited till the 28th of December. That year I became an orphan—well, that's what it felt like—at age 34. (I know there are so many others who have lost both parents much younger than me, but you feel so alone.)

This time, it was different. This time, I could have fallen apart; I wouldn't have in front of Joe Public, not in front of my children, but privately I allowed myself a bit, usually with my beloved dog. I sobbed, I cried, I screamed, and I ate. But I worked through it a bit better, but maybe not by much. I didn't have the previous pressures. But I did still have a full-time job, a family, and a house to run; they depended on me.

Give yourself a day, became my mantra.

Allow yourself the day to feel sorry for yourself, feel sad, feel angry, feel aggrieved, feel all those feelings, but also allow yourself to feel the love and guidance you had for all that time, the happiness and support, the underpinning that makes you able to go on. A day doesn't seem long; it's not. Sometimes a day didn't quite cut it; sometimes it was a week or longer, but in my mind, I kept telling myself a day.

I've experienced grief suddenly, and I've watched someone suffer.

My experience was that suddenly I suffered more; however, the person I loved did not. So, if there is a choice, I wouldn't want my loved one to suffer.

Grief, it's the hardest thing ever to go through. It's so unique to every person. What's right for one person may be entirely wrong for another.

My grief left me in my birth family of just myself and my brother. We have both been very different in our approach. He finds comfort in going to the graveside; I do not. I go on the days society would deem me to do so, Mother's Day, Father's Day, birthdays, etc.; however, it only upsets me; there is no comfort in it for me. Initially, he went slightly off the rails (understandably with my Mum) I just did what had to be done.

They tell you that grief gets easier with time, and to a certain point, I would agree. It's not the passage of time, though, but more the acceptance of your new reality.

I do understand that to have suffered with grief due to loss is from the love, guidance, and support you have previously had. So, is it a part of life we have to come to expect? It will be so different for every individual due to their circumstances and lived experiences.

My husband tells me that he will never feel the same way regarding the loss of his parents as I have done with mine. He says that currently his parents are in their eighties; they have done the circle of life; they have seen their children grow up and have families of their own, and they have even been lucky enough to see those families even have their own.

He thinks he will be okay in grief. I currently just say to him that we will cross that bridge when we come to it.

All I can say is I have a 100% success rate at getting through all the bad times so far, and I will continue to do so. I try my very hardest to be positive and grateful.

Some days are easier than others.

A Grief

"Everyone can master a grief, but he that has it."
~William Shakespeare, Much Ado About Nothing~

Growing Through the Love

by Jenny Ledwidge

My first life-impacting period of grief began in 2008 [1] when my lovely Mom was diagnosed with Parkinson's disease and Lewy body dementia. [2] She was a vibrant, passionate, loving, intelligent, fiercely independent Irish matriarch. She began showing symptoms about 2 years before we could get a diagnosis. I had noticed her appearing absent, facial expressions diminished, and she was not engaging as she used to. She was initially diagnosed with anxiety and depression.

Once we finally had a correct diagnosis [3], looking back, fear, disbelief, and problem-solving were my go-tos. I am a trained nurse and now recognise my nursing was my coping mechanism. What could I do to help Mom? What could I do to ease her suffering? Who can I ask for help and support? I researched, emailed, and phoned a plethora of experts to help. On reflection, I was in denial. By busying myself to help Mom, I was pushing the emotions down, as it was just too painful to face. [4]

I feel I need to say here that I do not believe that there are just 5 stages of grief, and in my experience, and people I have shared my grief journey with, there is no order to the stages identified by Kubler Ross (1969). Grief is messy, inconvenient, and overwhelming. The pain takes your breath away. My cousin describes grief as *'a boot in the fanny!'*

It is unexpected and hurts like hell!

When Mom first died on October 30th, 2020, during the pandemic, I had physical pain. [5] I felt like an orphan. I wondered who I was without Mom, where I belonged in the world.

Funeral arrangements were also affected, making it harder for people to say goodbye to loved ones in the way they would have liked. We had a restriction of 30 people, who had to socially distance and wear masks at the funeral.

Although I grieved and continue to do so, from the moment Mom died, I believe that I grieved slowly from the time Mom became ill, and I repeatedly grieved every time I saw Mom, every time I saw a decline, and watched her mind and body ravished by this cruel disease.

I felt a lot of anger. *Why, Mom, why is this happening to her?* When Mom died, I felt such anger towards people. I couldn't understand how the world kept moving. When my Mom was no longer in it!!

I remember, and it still happens now, when the tsunami of pain hits, I feel like I will die from the pain; I try to resist it. If you can let it out, do. It is also very normal to resist the pain, so do not force it; your mind and body are trying to protect you and will sometimes block out some of the pain. I try to accept and sit with the pain now and let it pass through me as much as I can. [6]

I thought I would feel some relief for Mom when she died, because of the long journey her illness had taken and the devastating toll it took on the person she was. However, I did not feel relief. I felt complete shock. As if I wasn't expecting her to die. For her, I was glad that she had peace after 12 years of this horrific disease, but I was still overwhelmed with losing her, but I have learned to build a life around that, mostly. I felt deep, deep sadness for the woman she was, and I still do. I felt regret going back to my teenage years, the arguments we had, the time when I was too busy. What I wouldn't give to slow down and cherish every single moment of her.[7] I felt guilt; whatever I tried to do to help support Mom, nothing felt enough. I also felt guilty because watching Mom go through this was no life for her, and I wondered many times during her living with Lewy body dementia and Parkinson's disease if her just slipping into a peaceful sleep would be better for her.

I have learned so much about myself and changing my expectations.

Some friends may back away; grief makes some people uncomfortable, and not everyone knows how to handle you. We are not the same person we once were; forgive them, accept them, remember them for who they were to you before this, and love them for that. It is hard for us all. I believe I now have more compassion and empathy and a deeper understanding of the pain and despair grief creates.

Take care of yourself; we have one life. There is no ending to the grief journey, merely building a new life around it. I'd like to say that it is ok to be angry that they died; that is normal. Just try not to hold on to the anger, and at times, if you direct it at someone else, acknowledge that, apologise, and ask for support. People will say things that will upset you, but generally, they do not mean to. I have discovered the importance of not expecting anyone to feel exactly how I feel and not minimising how others feel. I believe that the bad stuff makes you appreciate the good stuff even more; there's learning from the bad stuff. That's not to say that we could all do without the awful, painful, life-altering events that change us. Often in these times, and for me, it certainly was true that avoidance is a go-to because it hurts so much. Take good care of yourself.[8]

I remember when Mom died; for a long time I couldn't visualise who my mom was before she became so ill. It took months. Now, I dream of her so often as her well, healthy, feisty self. I feel so grateful to have these dreams of her and feel her comfort as if she were right there next to me. Although, I feel a fresh wave of pain when I wake up and realise it was a dream and not my reality. I often feel her presence. I can't see her or hear her in the physical sense, but I feel her as if she were whispering in my ear, standing behind me, guiding me and helping me to decide about things I am struggling with and sending me strength when I feel I have none left.

Whilst sorting the funeral and other mountains of necessities, I remember searching for signs of Mom. I couldn't bear to not see her again. I stared at the sky for hours and hours, looking for signs: rainbows, cloud shapes, robins, and feathers. I sat staring at the mirror, talking to her, looking for her to appear. I had candles lit constantly. I felt so dismayed I couldn't see her. My grief was blocking any connections I may feel to her.

This is my personal journey, and we all have our own beliefs. There are still things that I cannot face yet, such as watching our wedding video, because Mom and Clare are both very much alive there.

My Lovely sister Clare was 10 years older than me, my big sister. She died very suddenly from sepsis on the 4th of November 2021. The event came out of the blue, and only 12 months after losing Mom. I got a call on my way to work from my sister-in-law, and had I not been already en route to work, I would not have made it in time to say goodbye. The hospital was a short distance from my work. As awful as it was, I feel privileged to have been with her in her last moments.

Clare had the kindest heart and the sharpest wit I have ever known. She was so clever and oblivious to how much her laugh filled a room with joy. It was infectious; you could not help but end up with tears of laughter running down your face when in Clare's presence. If Clare could, she would drop everything immediately to help you. She would give you her last breath, her last penny, her last mouthful of food. Possessions meant nothing to Clare. She loved nothing more than the sunshine on her face and the sand beneath her feet. Her clumsy ways, which I have certainly inherited, would cause hysterics. There is no one quite like Clare in our lives now.

Covid restrictions during the times of Mom's and Clare's last months and their deaths meant that we as a family, and many people in the world, were often isolated and coping alone with their feelings and dealing with the practicalities of death over Zoom calls or alone. All of this has affected how we, and so many people, have been able to process grief, loss, and bereavement. For many, it has made the process more difficult, complicated, and traumatic.[9]

Moments do also haunt me about Clare. Could I have done anything to change the outcome? Why didn't I see her more before she died? Would I have noticed anything to prevent this if I had seen her more? It was 2021, and COVID restrictions were still in place. This meant I prioritised my immediate family by minimising contact with anyone else outside my home. As we had my gorgeous newborn grandson living with us at the time, that made us all extra cautious.

I had flashbacks a lot after I saw Clare die. I relived those moments for a long time.

I noticed feeling a lot of panic around my loved ones after both Mom and Clare died.[10] I remember a time when my husband Martyn was a little late home from work a few months after Clare died, and I tried to call to check he was ok. His phone said no service. I immediately catastrophised the worst possible outcome. This is another very common emotion to experience after someone has died.[11]

Some days, I felt I could not lift my head above the cover of the duvet.

One of the most common elements of dealing with grief is a strong feeling of sadness. It might be persistent over days or weeks, or it might only appear at certain moments, or it might appear out of nowhere. It can feel unbearable. I don't allow myself to do this very often, but some days, I literally have felt rooted to the bed, unable to move.

It hurt too much.[12]

What did I do to help myself after each death?

When memories popped up of Mom or times when I would have asked her questions, I wrote them down. [13] I bought a journal and wrote to Mom as if she were there. I found this very comforting. I made a playlist of Mom's and Clare's favourite songs. I baked Mom's favourite meals and made a recipe book for her specialities, and I still do. I did many photo collages of Mom and Clare all around the house. I also created a shrine of them both on my bedside table. At the time, it brought me a lot of comfort. I put this away only a short time ago, as it no longer felt helpful to me.

I walked a lot. I wandered around graveyards and sat on benches, just lost and dazed. I began baking, listening, and creating playlists of Irish music, Mom's favourite songs. I found a strong connection with my Irish family and childhood cousins. I took time off work. The world was moving too fast for me, and I wasn't ready to join it. I had grief counselling. [14] I found this so helpful both after losing Mom and Clare. I use the word loss, because it feels like that to me; however, I appreciate that some people will not view it in the way I do.

Grief is a very personal thing, so I apologise if this word is unhelpful for anyone. Grief counselling gave me a safe place to offload about how I felt each week to help process the rainbow of emotions that continued to change and evolve from minute to minute some days.

I joined a wonderful place called *'The Happiness Club,'* and 3 weeks after Mom died, I began training to be a Happiness Club trainer. This was an amazing business that I discovered in the summer of 2020, before Mom died. I found it online, quite by accident, and it changed my whole path. I began learning tools and techniques in mindfulness, meditation, thought challenging, relaxation, and journaling, to name but a few. I learned how to present these tools so that someday I could share them with other organisations, businesses, and schools. I am eternally grateful.

As part of the Happiness Club, I also joined a course called *'Lyfe' (Love Yourself First Experience)*. This was an amazing course of self-discovery and opened the world of meditation, full moon rituals, and further journaling to me. I found it a great way to release a lot of emotions, and on full moon rituals, burning anything I had written that I wanted to let go of was very cleansing.

I trained to be an EFT practitioner. I again found this very healing, calm, safe, and accepting. I am so grateful to have learned those skills.

Sometimes your mind won't allow you rest to meditate, releasing emotions in that way, so EFT, or tapping as it is commonly known, can allow you to release emotions. As a nurse and someone who is always **doing**, I found this worked well for me. I remember one day; we were asked to come up with a memory of food. I thought of hot buttered toast. I had not expected that this would release such powerful emotions of grief. I had chosen this, as it made me think at that time of comfort, the smell, the taste of butter, of finishing night shifts, and it tasting like the best thing ever before climbing into bed. However, as I began tapping, I began to weep uncontrollably. I realised my mind had gone to where the love of hot buttered toast came from, which was Mom. I released a lot of emotion that day and many times after in a safe space.[15]

I also became interested in crystals thanks to Martyn's lovely friend, who I had several conversations with after Mom and Clare died. The world of crystals became very comforting to me. I surrounded our house.[16]

Although it did result in a rather embarrassing incident on my first day back to work after Mom died when I put crystals in my bra as protection, and when I bent down to empty a patient catheter, the crystals fell out on the recovery unit floor in front of my colleague. I scooped them up and rapidly put them away! This was the last time I put crystals in my bra!

I used a lot of breathing techniques, as I felt super anxious and on high alert. I felt utter panic and fear that something terrible would happen to someone else in my family/friend circle. Breathing techniques often got me to the next moment.[17]

Mindfulness has been a great healer for me. I have learned to live every moment, to be grateful for every moment, and to do things if I can that I always wanted to do, to not be afraid to try new things, new experiences, meet new people, change jobs, travel, and love fiercely, because you never know what is around the next corner. It may be good stuff, it may be terrible stuff, it may be blah stuff; grab on to moments and cherish them. I feel privileged to feel the sun on my face, to see sunsets, rainbows, clouds, rain, and snow. I appreciate things that Mom could no longer do for herself when she was ill: to walk, to see the sea, to talk, and to laugh. I have learned to appreciate things I never thought of before; tasting really gorgeous food, the feeling of a hot shower, and the ability to stand in a shower and wash myself is a gift.

What I have learned from mindfulness is to let go of stuff. I learned that holding on to anger, grief, and pain; holding grudges; and holding resentment and regret all hurt us and only us. It doesn't mean you can't feel it. Acknowledge it, journal it, but don't hang on to it; **whatever works for you.**

Mindfulness can be gardening, showering, walking, exercising, seeing, knitting, baking, planting seeds, walking the dog, music, or whatever being in the moment means to you and works for you. We live so much in the past or future; don't miss the now; it is precious. Mindfulness helps us observe our emotions. It's like having a mental anchor, keeping us steady in the storm of sadness.[18]

As I write this, it has been 2 and a half years since Clare died, and mostly I still feel utter disbelief. I feel it is only just beginning to sink in sometimes that Clare is no longer on this earth.

Out of the blue, my triggers for Clare have so far been music, certain songs, playing pool in a bar, and randomly at my husband's Christmas work party, someone who looked nothing like Clare, but her mannerisms were very similar; she then used a phrase that Clare would have said. *"How beautiful is that?"*. Clare would always compliment people, places, and situations, but sadly never recognised how amazing she was.

New Year 2021, it snowed for just one night; my daughter Rosa and I went outside and made snow angels and walked and played in the snow at 10 pm on the 2nd of January 2021. By 9 am the next day, the snow was all gone. I felt so glad we grabbed onto that moment.

Don't wait until you retire; don't wait for the big events; plan small things to bring you joy; it doesn't have to cost money; find your joy where you live; create your joy in your home; adapt your life to give you the sense of peace you crave.

Don't wait for it to happen to you.

Inner peace, I get it now; find peace in your mind, accept all the emotions, and let them pass through you; holding onto them hurts you physically and mentally.[19]

I left nursing in September 2022 to complete a master's and become a CBT practitioner.

After being a nurse for 20 years, I needed a change. The training was intense. I have learned a great deal, but now, on reflection, I took on too much too soon after losing Mom and Clare. I threw myself into training, learning new things, and spirituality. It was my coping mechanism, and now I am choosing to have a break in the academic field.

I now recognise I was trying to fill the void of Clare and Mom dying by being constantly busy and distracted. I cannot fill the void of their deaths and the fact that they are no longer here in the physical sense on earth. I know I need to give my mind and body time to slow down and heal a little more from all that has been over the last 3 and a half years.

This year, I started classes in Pilates and yoga. I have found both so helpful, both physically and emotionally. It requires concentration and balance and can be a physical challenge. The many things I have used to help me begin to heal and grow are not prescriptive; we all have to find our own way.

A deep hole exists where Mom and Clare were. However, the love I have for my family deepens every day and helps the healing process. I have a newfound appreciation and gratitude for my family and how precious they are to me; how lucky I am to have them in my life. How grateful I am to have the most patient, kind, caring, loving man as my husband, my amazing, beautiful kids, and the light in all our lives, Logan!

Logan, my grandson who is now 2 and a half, is pure joy, pure love, pure wonder.

Grief is not a stationary journey; it has constant ups and downs and is an unpredictable path, sometimes with changes in emotion from hour to hour.

The day I found out Hayley and Jacob were having Logan, something shifted in me; it was just after the first Mother's Day after Mom died. I hit a big low this day. The pain was palpable. A few days later, Hayley and Jacob handed us a card with a scan photo in it. I remember that feeling of utter joy at that moment. Logan brings so much joy and peace to us all. I talk about this grief from my perspective, as we all had our own relationship with Mom and Clare, but I feel it is important to acknowledge that my kids also felt such pain and grief over Mom and Clare. It has rocked and changed all our lives, and we are all finding our own ways to live through this, day by day, and take the grief as it comes, when it comes, often with no invitation!

I believe that this year I have felt more deep sadness with the realisation and some acceptance that both Mom and Clare are no longer on this earth physically.

I have stopped resisting the pain to some extent.

I am also learning not to 'fill the void.' I am creating as many lovely, exquisite moments as I can and trying to embrace the many beautiful people and opportunities that I am lucky enough to have around me.

I have felt utterly drained and exhausted this year more than ever, after chasing ways to 'fix' how I felt and avoid the reality.

By letting it in and accepting this new reality, it has allowed the tiredness of it all to come through. But it has also given room for a little less anxiety by going with the flow a little more. I now try to see what the world sends my way and stop attempting to prevent and cushion things that may or may not happen.

I guess the biggest learning here is to take nothing for granted, to know only I can find my way through this journey, but with the many recommended activities, professional help, hobbies, love, and support around me and by allowing myself to adapt, grow, go with the flow, and accept.

The love is still there for Mom and Clare as strong as ever, and the emotional and spiritual connection is still there, but for me, there is a gap at the table at Christmas where they used to be. The Christmas table where my sisters, brother, sister-in-law, stepdad, our children, and partners all gathered. We have all grieved and continue to do so in our own very personal and private way.

One photo I will be forever grateful for is one of us all at such an event, capturing each of us naturally, with my Mom at the centre.

However, I have my own Christmas table now, with my own beautiful family. I am so lucky to have that and I can create new memories while cherishing and smiling when I think about the old ones. I feel as if I am walking in Mom's shoes every day, and I imagine how she must have felt with each life event. I see clearly the depth of love that came from Clare.

Mostly, I am forever grateful for my beautiful friends, family, and especially Martyn, Jacob, Barney, Rosa, Hayley, and, of course, Logan!

"I feel privileged to share my insights by contributing a chapter to this beautiful book, offering guidance, understanding, and hope to others.""I met my wonderful husband, Martyn, in Mallorca, where we later married. He is from Falkirk, Scotland, and together *we have built a loving family. I am forever grateful for Martyn, Jacob, Barney, Hayley, Logan, and Rosa—who are the loves of my life. My children, Jacob, Barney, and Rosa, are my greatest achievements, and my family remains my greatest blessing."*

Thank you for reading.

1. American Psychological Association. (2020, January 1). Grief: Coping with the loss of your loved one. *Https://Www.apa.org*. https://www.apa.org/topics/grief

2. https://www.parkinson.org/understanding-parkinsons/non-movement-symptoms/dementia/lewy-bodies

3. www.alzheimers.org.uk/get-support/help-dementia-care/grief-loss-and-bereavement?gad_source=1&gclid=EAIaIQobChMIhqWgmdHihgMVsZJQBh2cLwc5EAAYASAAEgI5MPD_BwE&gclsrc=aw.ds

4. https://www.ncbi.nlm.nih.gov/books/NBK507885/#:~:text=Denial%20is%20a%20common%20defense

5. https://www.mariecurie.org.uk/information/grief/physical-symptoms

6. https://www.helpguide.org/mental-health/grief/coping-with-grief-and-loss

7. https://pmc.ncbi.nlm.nih.gov/articles/PMC4018291/

8. https://pmc.ncbi.nlm.nih.gov/articles/PMC5482544/

9. https://www.ataloss.org/pages/faqs/category/coronavirus-pandemic?gad_source=1&gclid=EAIaIQobChMI2fj92oudiQMVpJZQBh0JmTAOEAAYASAAEgJvJPD_BwE%20[Accessed%2020%20Oct.%202024].

10. https://www.mindwell-leeds.org.uk/myself/how-life-experiences-can-affect-us/bereavement-and-loss/coping-with-flashbacks-a-during-bereavement/

11. https://www.getselfhelp.co.uk/

12. https://kerryhowells.com/how-can-we-find-gratitude-in-the-midst-of-grief/

13. https://www.cruse.org.uk/understanding-grief/managing-grief/grief-journal/

14. https://primrosehospice.org/

15. https://thelossfoundation.org/triggers-in-grief/

16. https://www.centreofexcellence.com/

17. https://www.frontiersin.org/journals/human-neuroscience/articles/10.3389/fnhum.2018.00353/full

18. https://www.nhs.uk/mental-health/self-help/tips-and-support/mindfulness/

19. https://www.mindful.org/mindfulness-for-grief-and-loss/#:~:text=Mindfulness%20is%20all%20about%20paying.

Grief Is Tough

by Laura Penn

Grief is tough.

Let's not pretend it isn't.

But it has a purpose.

Loss is such a small word for something so big. I have experienced plenty of different types of loss in my life: pets, possessions, places, positions, and people.

Death was probably the easiest.

That may sound odd, and I'm not saying that the deaths of my parents and friends were fun, but the people that I have loved and lost through death did not choose to leave me that way. I know if they had a say in it, they would still be here with me so I can celebrate them and their lives and all the good things that they gave me.

It was the loss that came from a choice that I found the most difficult.

The people who chose to leave.

My first boyfriend cheated on me.

My husband chose another woman.

They felt like rejection, and, yes; they hurt.

It was genuine grief.

It took me longer to get to the same place with those people, but I did eventually.

That is one thing I have learned; it may take longer to let go, but you get there in the end.

You do heal.

When you can bless all your losses, you have nailed it.

Another thing I've found is that loss is not always a bad thing.

It bloody feels like it at the time.... but give it time.

The losses I have experienced have always opened up new paths, ideas, and relationships that I would never have followed or experienced without going through the process of loss, grief, and renewal. And I am grateful. It took a while, but I got there.

I nailed it!

I'm not going to make light of that process; it is tough. There are times when I've not felt or behaved great. I choose not to dwell on those times. They happened, and I am grateful they did. I'd rather not go through them again, but they changed me, and I think for the better.

Therefore, surely grief is good.

Not at the time, I grant you, but eventually.

And if, at the time of grief, you can get perspective and know that *this too will pass* and something good will arise from it, surely that is a comfort.

I have no doubt I have losses yet to come, grief yet to feel, and the process to go through again, different but the same.

I hope that my experiences in the past will serve me well in coping with the emotions that inevitably accompany the journey, and I will realise that sunnier days and fun times are always ahead if you plan that journey and hold your head up while you travel.

Zooties

FROM MY HEART TO YOUR HEART

Zoot   Zoot   Zoot

My story behind grief

Anonymous

When Linda asked me to make some notes on my experience of grief, I thought it may not be relevant as it was so long ago now when I experienced it.

I lost both parents at an early age: my mother and best friend 37 years ago, and my father and hero 32 years ago.

Everyone copes differently with grief, and my work as an international investment adviser has revealed many examples of how people cope or do not cope.

I had one client who got in touch with me before anyone else when her husband died suddenly because she was completely lost and needed someone to hold her hand. Another client could not bear to pick up the phone for several weeks as she simply did not have the strength or courage. She was completely shattered by her experience.

My situation back in 1987 was perhaps a little different, and I have to this day carried the burden of whether I did the right thing or not. What I have had to live with is the wrong that I may have done to my family at the time.

My mother was an incredibly strong, independent, and proud lady.

A midwife and nursing officer extraordinaire. While in her hospital bed during her last days, a lady occupied the bed opposite her to whom she had delivered two children many years before. They not only visited their Mum but my Mum too.

So strong was my Mum, that she only shared her devastating news with me—that she had been told she had 3 months to live. *"I'm not scared,"* she said, *"and I have to ask you just for now that you keep this news to yourself. I do not want anyone—your father, your brothers, family, or friends—to know. The boys (my brothers) have such busy lives; I do not want them putting themselves out, travelling all this way to feel sorry for me. I have plenty of time to tell them nearer the end."*

She went home from the hospital and wrote a letter to us all, prepared her funeral, and made the house and garden perfect so that Dad wouldn't have to do anything to it for a while. He was not well himself at this stage, but she told me he's like a creaking gate and will carry on swinging.

He did, for a further 5 years.

After only a week or so of being home, her leg began to swell, and she got admitted back into the hospital. We went to see her, and she seemed ok and made me promise still not to tell anyone.

That night I went home with Dad, and we stopped for a pint on the way back. Dad was missing Mum, and, for some reason, I was feeling extremely anxious about leaving her. We went to bed, and then at 1.00 am, the phone rang, asking us to go quickly to the hospital as Mum was in her final stages of life. I frantically tried to get Dad out of bed, get him dressed, and get him into the car, but he was disoriented and so slow it took us an hour to get there. By that time, it was too late; she was already on her journey.

The nursing sister said she was very peaceful and that she'd held her. Inside my head, I screamed that it should have been me holding her, but Dad's fumbling about had cost me that.

The shock to my brothers was enormous, as you can imagine, but they too were filled with their own anger, in particular one brother who guessed that I knew how poorly she was and hadn't shared that with them. I had stolen time with Mum from them, and they would never get that back.

I tried to occupy myself running around, making sure Dad was ok; even though I was angry, I thought that focusing on everything else might ease my brother's anger too.

The guilt and anguish remained, although my anger turned into empathy for Dad. He was totally lost without her and wholly dependent on support.

It was only by accident a couple of years later that I found out that one of my team members at work was a spiritual healer. He sensed something in me and questioned what burden I was hanging onto. I explained that not being there when my Mum died and holding onto Mum's secret had backfired on my family.

He put his arm around me and told me that my mother had every right to end her days the way she wanted. In fact, she probably knew she had only weeks to live, not months, and that secret she took to the grave.

How could I have betrayed her? It was her choice.

He then went on to say that her being alone at her final breath would also have been her choice. She wanted to go when none of us were around her. That was just how she'd planned it. Some people need you there, and some do not want you there. We have no control over that.

Five years later, Dad was admitted to the hospital and suffered a stroke, which we knew he'd likely not recover from.

This time I was open with my family; he didn't want any secrets, and my brothers didn't either. So we all arranged to meet at his bedside as quickly as we could all get there from our various locations. One brother was missing, and Dad was slipping away but hung on with his dear life until he arrived, and within the half hour, he slipped off on his journey while we all held his hand.

How different this time was, and I could see clearly how both my parents had had their last moments exactly as they had chosen.

What I didn't realise in my grief on both counts was that I had to finalise matters just as I thought they would have wanted them. Not to take responsibility for it, I got lost in doing what I believed was the right thing.

Probably it was only then that I was aware I wanted to grieve and felt at ease. My relationship with the one brother took 8 years to repair; he had to grieve himself, as he was Mum's pride and joy. He owed his excellent education to my mother's determination. We are all blessed now with a healthy, happy outlook, and he continually sends me brilliant jokes as we share similar senses of humour! All my brothers and I love to talk about how special our parents were; we all have different stories to share.

It was the acceptance that everyone has a different angle on grief that released me, and there is no right or wrong way; there just is! It helps to understand and be mindful that we all need to grieve in some way; it's finding out which way that helps and is the key.

Adding to this, and something again, that is a different angle, albeit maybe a rather odd one for some to accept. Once I came to terms with my grieving process, I was speaking to a friend who said to look out for signs from them. After losing his mother in tragic circumstances, he told me that once, when he was feeling troubled, he had seen a robin in the garden, and then it became a regular thing. It wasn't the winter; it was summer, and he does not live in the UK; he lives in a hot climate! He liked to imagine this was his Mum flying in to say hello, and he always found it quite comforting.

I then recalled lots of dreams that featured my Mum in them. She was still alive in them, and although ill, she came and joined me for things like shopping and work events I was running. It was magical seeing her, and it always lifted my spirits with the feeling that she was still there. Occasionally I still have them, but rather than try to analyse them, I merely enjoy them.

My father, on the other hand, had to do things a bit more boldly and mischievously. The first time something odd happened was when I was on the phone with my friend one evening after putting my son to bed. Whilst we were chatting in the hallway, his remote-control car, his favourite toy, which my father's best friend had bought him, began moving across the kitchen floor and into the hallway. It really spooked me, and my husband thought it was hilarious, saying it was simply a loose connection.

Believing what he said, I was on the phone the following week with the same friend when it began again. This time it reversed back to the lounge where his toys were situated, and I absolutely froze with fear. Seeking advice from my old team member at work, he asked me who was mischievous, and that was very easy to answer. Seeing my stress and fear, however, he just said to tell Dad, "I don't think it's funny," and to stop. I must admit I went through that exercise but didn't want signals from him to stop; I was fearful that he'd go.

Being a heavy smoker until the day he passed, I then received the smell of fresh smoke on many occasions. It would be in the car, in my house, at work, and even near my son's bed. No one else could smell it until one day I heard from the people who had bought my father's house and renovated it. They had put on a conservatory from the lounge, but now and then had to open the doors because it smelled like someone had been smoking there. Their son told his Mum, *"It's probably the man that sits at the end of my bed during the night,"* but he was a nice man, so he wasn't scared.

Those reminders of my father have since dwindled as life has moved on and the memories fade... until a few weeks ago. I was visiting my brothers back in the UK andI had a very brief reminder. A strong smell of smoke filled the room even though Dad knew my brother is a huge anti-smoker. Made me smile all day long.

Grief is just Love with no place to go

Jamie Anderson

"Grief, I've learned, is really love.

It's all the love you want to give but cannot give. The more you loved someone, the more you grieve. All of that unspent love gathers up in the corners of your eyes and in that part of your chest that gets empty and hollow feeling. The happiness of love turns to sadness when unspent.

Grief is just love with no place to go."

~ Anderson, J. (2014) As the Lights Wink Out. All My Loose Ends, 25th March 2014~

Grief is the process by which we manage to live serenely with the loss of someone or something

by Valerie Haesen (Valou)

For me, grief is the process by which we manage to live serenely with the loss of someone or something.

Throughout my personal development, I've come to realise that grieving becomes easier when we adopt a vision of the acceptance of the world and look at each event from a positive angle; in other words, the lesson we can learn from it to help us grow.

We're all just passing through on this earth, or in someone else's life, and I'm firmly convinced that this passage, however long it lasts, is a learning path for our personal evolution.

Everything that happens to us has a reason in this journey, and when we have this point of view, we know that even the hardest things we will go through exist to reach this new, grown-up version of ourselves. It's in this sense that a difficult event can be seen in a 'positive' way, as a vector for personal evolution.

I'm currently going through grief, but this one differs from the others because it's anticipatory, i.e., I know that my father will leave within a specific timeframe because he's ill with no possibility of recovery. You'll tell me that this is the case for everyone; we will all die one day, but we all know that these moments allow us to take a break from the daily grind of our lives to appreciate what is.

I could resist the idea and take offence, but acceptance and going with the flow make the journey less painful.

I'm grateful that this illness has been announced and that it allows us to prepare for future absences by taking full and conscious advantage of the time we have left together.

Yes, it's going to be a difficult road; I'll have moments of sadness and fear. *What am I going to do without him?* He's my *'guardian,'* the one I can count on, the one who will help me get out of any complicated situation… but in the end, having accompanied me and taught me about life over all these years, I know that everything he has taught me is inside of me, and I'll draw on that or from those who will be at my side to move forward.

The other aspect of grief, absence, I've seen differently in recent years because I'm convinced that physical absence from this world doesn't mean permanent absence.

My friend Christine left suddenly, and there was nothing I could do to prepare myself for her absence. I wept for her, looked back, and remembered her laughter, her joviality, and her outbursts that made her **'HER,'** and I thanked the universe for having put me in her path. After the church ceremony, a butterfly landed near us, as if to say I'm here... that butterfly came back at the wedding of a mutual friend. When I'm in the car sometimes, I suddenly feel a wave of emotion run through me, and I know that it's her beside me, that the song playing on the radio, *"Il suffira d'un signe,"* is her... reminding me that she's always by my side.

Yes, I feel sad; I live it; I allow myself to be downcast for a while.

This time it allows us to refocus on ourselves and, via our internal dialogues, accept what we've been given by becoming aware of all that this relationship has brought us, that it has allowed us to grow, and that if we pay attention, these parents/friends have just passed over to the other side and are accompanying us differently today.

Their signs will be their way of letting us know that they are still there and that they will continue to guide us.

In short, mourning is a period of introspection during which we allow ourselves to feel our emotions, accept the physical absence of the person who has gone, and welcome their presence in a different way while being grateful for the traces left in our lives.

Weep

William Shakespeare

"To weep is to make less the depth of grief."
   1592 Richard. Henry VI Part Three, act 2, sc.1, l.85-6~

Transforming Grief into Hope

by Deidre MaGuire

According to the British Mental Health Foundation, one in three of us is suicidal.

Because of stress, 75% of us experience feelings of being unable to cope. These statistics highlight the pervasive struggle many face daily, often in silence.

It is in this context of hidden battles and personal pain that my own journey of grief and hope begins.

So I wonder how you would feel if you got the phone call to tell you that someone you love very deeply had just taken their own life. That's what happened to me.

My darling father, my hero, my mentor—outwardly a successful and generous businessman, but inwardly unable to cope with the pain from his past, gradually, he fell victim to daily alcohol abuse, and in the end, a tortured soul, he went with the only option left to him and took his own life.

I remember the call. I remember my blasé response to my sister-in-law when she nervously muttered that my Dad was *"in the river"*—just another alcohol-induced insanity drama—the new norm of recent times.

As the full force of the end of my life with my father in it hit home, my world shattered.

I had made it my mission to save my Dad, to be there for him in his darkest moments, and nothing had worked.

As I stood by the open coffin, staring at his finally motionless face, the emotional stun gun of the private pain and the public shame of suicide zapped my body relentlessly.

When the coffin disappeared into the cold January earth, I had only one truth left.

I had failed.

The lowest point of my life. *(Do you know someone who's ever felt just like that?)*

But, what if the lowest point is actually the turning point?

The days, weeks, and months that followed my father's death were like an emotional blur, hurtling from confusion to anger to sadness to even my own suicidal thoughts, but always one constant:

The search. The search for answers.

Why did my father have to die? Is death the only ultimate solution to emotional pain? Are we forever doomed to be trapped by the trauma of our past?

In the initial stages of grief, it's easy to feel overwhelmed and lost. The pain is so intense that it consumes your every thought, your every breath. It feels like you're drowning in a sea of sorrow, with no land in sight. Yet, even in those darkest moments, there's a desperate flicker of light—a tiny, almost imperceptible spark of hope. Life is always trying to make sense of itself.

Though it certainly does not feel like it.

Like the famous book *"Man's Search for Meaning,"* written by Victor Frankl, a Jewish psychologist kept alive in Auschwitz, the human spirit searches for understanding and for a way out of the abyss.

Slowly, the pain began to subside.

And then came the purpose.

I became a life coach, a master practitioner of my trade. I had helped myself first, and now I was helping others. I had turned my personal journey into my professional passion.

I remember the first time I got paid by a client. I pinned the check to the notice board and said out loud to my father, *"What do you think of that,*

Da?" I swear to God, I heard him say, *"Deirdre, have I taught you nothing about the cash?"*

Turning my grief into a purpose was definitely not an overnight transformation. It was a gradual process, filled with setbacks and breakthroughs. I had no clue then, but each step forward was a testament to the resilience of the human spirit.

I started small, helping friends and family members navigate their own emotional challenges. With each success, my confidence grew, and so did my ambition. I enrolled in courses, read countless books, sought mentorship, trained, and studied neuro-linguistic programming. The more I learnt, the more I realised the depth of my father's pain (and my own) and the reasons behind his tragic decision. This understanding brought a sense of peace and purpose and also a renewed determination to help others avoid a similar fate.

And then a weirdly special gift arrived, and it was not from Amazon.

A lump on my neck, a cancer diagnosis.

What I remember most is not the solemn face of the doctor as he declared that surgery would be first, followed by chemotherapy, then radiation. What I remember most is not the possibility that I was going to die.

What I remember most is that I had not lived.

Stress—the posh word for fear—had been driving my life, just like my father before me.

Change had to happen.

Now was the time for me to put everything I had learned about emotional intelligence and personal power to the test. Cancer was giving me the chance to put my money where my mouth was. So I did. Cancer gave me the chance to say yes to the surgery and no to the chemotherapy and radiation. The biggest NO to all those limiting beliefs that had been driving me all my life. And the biggest YES to my truth is that you absolutely can have control over your mind, your body, and, most of all, your spirit.

The cancer diagnosis was a pivotal moment in my life. It forced me to confront my mortality and evaluate the way I had been living.

For too long, I had been driven by fear—fear of failure, fear of judgement, fear of not being enough. This fear had manifested in stress, which in turn had taken a toll on my health. The cancer was a wake-up call, a stark reminder that life is precious and fleeting. It was an invitation to live more authentically, to align my actions with my values, and to prioritise my well-being.

All that was twelve years ago.

Today, I'm a world-class mind wellness expert. I help people get happier. I show them how to see and then change the patterns of thinking that are blinding them to their emotional intelligence and blocking them from who they really are.

Today, I've clocked up thousands of hours and worked with hundreds of people all over the world.

And what I know for sure is this: there is no need to die. There is no need to stay stuck in those patterns of painful thinking that are narrowing your vision, so emotional suicide daily is your only option left.

All that's required is a desire, a decision, and a commitment to change. And change is just unfamiliar. Otherwise, it wouldn't be a change. What's required is for you to go to the edge of your comfort zone. Because you know something. That's where change lives. In the words of my favourite client, *"Let's get this party started."*

Reflecting on this journey, I realise how profoundly grief and hope are intertwined.

Grief is a process that shakes us to our core, but it also has the potential to ignite a transformation within us. It's not about getting over the loss, but about growing through it. Grief teaches us to cherish life, to seek purpose, and to find strength we never knew we had. It challenges us to confront our deepest fears and, in doing so, opens the door to profound personal growth.

My father's death was a turning point, a catalyst for change. It forced me to confront the patterns of pain and fear that had governed my life and to seek a different path. In the depths of my despair, I found a new purpose. I discovered the power of emotional intelligence and the importance of taking control of my mind and spirit. This journey of grief led me to a place of hope where I could help others navigate their own struggles.

Cancer was another turning point, a test of everything I had learnt. It was a stark reminder of the importance of living authentically and fearlessly. By embracing the challenge and rejecting the limitations imposed by fear, I found a deeper sense of purpose and a renewed commitment to my own well-being.

Today, I am driven by a mission to help others find hope and strength in their darkest moments. I believe that we all have the capacity to transform our grief into a source of power and inspiration. It requires a willingness to confront our pain, to seek out the lessons it holds, and to embrace the journey of healing and growth.

Grief is not just a personal journey; it is also a universal one. Everyone, at some point in their life, experiences loss. Whether it is the death of a loved one, the end of a relationship, or the loss of a job, grief is a natural response to significant change. Understanding this universality can be comforting. It reminds us that we are not alone in our suffering. Others have walked this path before us and have emerged stronger and wiser.

One of the most profound lessons I've learnt is the importance of community in the healing process. Grief can be isolating, making us feel like we are alone in our pain. But sharing our stories, our struggles, and our victories can create connections that heal. When I started speaking openly about my father's suicide and my cancer diagnosis, I was met with an outpouring of support. People from all walks of life reached out to share their own experiences and to offer words of encouragement. This sense of community was a lifeline, providing the strength I needed to keep moving forward.

In my work as a mind wellness expert, I emphasise the importance of emotional intelligence. This involves recognising and understanding our own emotions and those of others. It is about developing the skills to manage our emotions effectively and to respond to the emotions of others with empathy and compassion. Emotional intelligence is not just a professional skill; it is a life skill. It helps us navigate the complexities of human relationships and build meaningful connections.

Another key aspect of my journey has been the practice of mindfulness. Mindfulness is about being present in the moment, fully engaging with our thoughts, feelings, and surroundings. It is about accepting our emotions without judgement and responding to them with kindness and compassion. Mindfulness has been a powerful tool in my healing process, helping me to manage stress, reduce anxiety, and improve my overall well-being.

Physical health is also a crucial component of emotional wellness. After my cancer diagnosis, I made significant changes to my lifestyle. I adopted a healthier diet, incorporated regular exercise into my routine, and made sure to get enough sleep. These changes had a profound impact on my physical and emotional health. They gave me the energy and resilience I needed to face the challenges ahead.

Spirituality has been another important element of my journey. For me, spirituality is about connecting with something greater than myself. It is about finding meaning and purpose in life and developing a sense of inner peace and harmony. This connection has been a source of strength and comfort, providing guidance and support in times of need.

As I reflect on my journey, I am filled with gratitude. Gratitude for the lessons I've learned, the people I've met, and the opportunities I've had to make a difference. I am grateful for the chance to transform my grief into a source of hope and inspiration for others. And I am grateful for the reminder that, even in our darkest moments, there is always a spark of light.

Grief is a journey, not a destination. It is a process of growth and transformation, of finding meaning and purpose in the face of loss. It is about embracing our pain and using it as a catalyst for change. It is about connecting with others and finding strength in a community. And most importantly, it is about finding hope. Hope that we can heal, that we can grow, and that we can find joy and fulfilment in life once again.

If you are struggling with grief, know that you are not alone. There is a community of people who understand your pain and who are here to support you. Reach out, share your story, and connect with others. Allow yourself to feel your emotions, to grieve, and to heal. And remember, even in your darkest moments, there is always a spark of hope.

So, let's get this party started. Let's embark on this journey of healing and growth together. Let's transform our grief into a source of strength and inspiration. Let's find hope in the face of loss and joy in the midst of sorrow. And let's live our lives with purpose, passion, and authenticity. Because, in the end, that is what life is all about.

Embracing the Journey

Grief is a complex and multifaceted emotion, one that weaves its way through every aspect of our lives. It touches our hearts, minds, bodies, and spirits, leaving no part of us unchanged. But within the depths of our sorrow lies the potential for profound transformation. By embracing our grief and allowing ourselves to fully experience it, we open the door to healing and growth.

In the years since my father's death and my cancer diagnosis, I have learned to view grief not as an enemy to be conquered but as a teacher to be heeded. Grief has taught me to appreciate the fleeting beauty of life, to cherish moments of joy and connection, and to find strength in vulnerability. It has shown me that true healing comes not from avoiding pain but from facing it head-on and allowing it to transform us.

One of the most powerful ways we can honour our grief is by giving it a voice. When we share our stories, we not only lighten our own burden but also offer comfort and hope to others who are struggling. Our experiences become a source of strength and inspiration, a testament to the resilience of the human spirit.

As a life coach, mentor, and mind wellness expert, I have had the privilege of witnessing countless stories of transformation. I have seen people rise from the ashes of their pain, find new purpose in their lives, and create meaningful connections with others. These stories are a reminder that, no matter how deep our grief, we are capable of healing and growth.

In my own journey, I have found solace in the simple act of being present. By grounding myself in the present moment, I can fully experience my emotions without being overwhelmed by them. Mindfulness practices such as meditation, deep breathing, and journaling have been invaluable tools in my healing process. They have helped me to cultivate a sense of inner peace and to navigate the ups and downs of life with grace and resilience.

Physical activity has also played a crucial role in my journey of healing. I am a very proud CrossFit athlete. *(Currently, the oldest in my gym!)* It reminds me of my strength and vitality and reinforces the importance of self-care.

Another key element of my healing journey has been the practice of gratitude. By focusing on the positive aspects of my life, I can shift my perspective and to find joy even in the midst of sorrow. Gratitude journaling, where I regularly write down things I am thankful for, has been a powerful practice in cultivating a sense of appreciation and contentment.

Spirituality, too, has been a guiding force in my journey. For me, spirituality is about connecting with a higher power, finding meaning in life's experiences, and developing a sense of inner peace. Whether through prayer, meditation, or simply spending time in nature, these practices help to ground me and provide a sense of purpose and direction.

As I look to the future, I am filled with hope. Hope for continued healing, for deeper connections, and for the opportunity to make a difference in the lives of others. I am committed to using my experiences to inspire and empower others, to help them navigate their own journeys of grief and growth, and to find hope and joy in their lives.

Grief is not an emotion or a feeling; it is an emotional, physical, mental, and spiritual process we experience as a reaction to a life event that causes us to feel deep anguish—a range of mixed but usually deeply sad and angry emotions—severe mental or physical pain, or suffering. This is usually related to the loss of a loved one or someone or something that leaves a huge gap in our life. I have found that many people hold grief in their body physically, mentally, and spiritually. They often do not know how to release it or embrace it.

For me, grief is not something you get over or move on from. For me, it is something that you grow through, and if you can find the gift in grief, well, that's when it becomes part of your life journey, and you look at it in a very different way. Grief is a journey; it is not a destination. We are not meant to remain there.

I know not everyone will have the same point of view as I have, and that's okay. That, in fact, is the reason I am writing this chapter.

My aim is to share my story in the hope that it will give people the strength to release their grief, grow through their grief, find solace and comfort again in their life, or even just simply to know that they are not alone.

As we move forward together, let us embrace our grief and allow it to transform us. Let us find hope in the face of loss and joy in the midst of sorrow.

And let us live our lives with purpose, passion, and authenticity.

Because, in the end, that is what life is all about.

Grief

by Lisa Ferris

The last time I switched my phone off was 31/7/2003. I switched it off and checked it in with my coat and bag. It was a Thursday night, and my boyfriend at the time came over from Belfast to visit me in Glasgow. He arrived earlier that day, and I picked him up and dropped him off at the hotel we were staying at for the weekend.

I went to see my Mum who was in the ICU and had been for a week.

I was close to not going to visit her during the visiting times as I was leaving it late, and the hospital was way on the other side of the city. But I did; I went. She was awake after having been in an induced coma for the week. She was awake and talking vividly about how thirsty she was and that she could drink dirty dishwater. She had been on a ventilator regulating her breathing. She then proceeded to tell me and my sister that she had some nice salty milk given to her by John. We did not know who she was referring to and wondered why she didn't say, doctor. As we walked away, having left the room, I turned round to wave at her once more, and she was waiting to wave back enthusiastically, glad I did, as that was the last time I saw her alive.

After partying in the club that night and walking out with my coat and bag, I switched on my phone, and many voicemails appeared. I listened to the first message; it was my Dad asking me where I was in a panicked voice and to call him as soon as I got this message. Another one came through more frantic from him, holding back tears and saying how he didn't want me to find out like this, but Mum had died, and he was in Glasgow looking for me.

I stopped dead in the street. Jamie stopped and looked at me. I couldn't speak. He started panicking; *"Lisa, what is it? What happened?"* I stared at him as my eyes filled with water at the realisation of the words I was about to say out loud. *"She's gone!"* *"Who's gone?"* Jamie asked confused. *"My Mum, she's dead!"* I called my Dad back immediately; he wasn't far away; he came and got us. I don't remember much, but he said everyone was at the hospital; they were all trying to get through to me.

Walking through the hospital in the early hours of the morning, having to be quiet whilst the other patients slept, was surreal. Seeing Mum stone-cold laid out was even more surreal. I couldn't understand; I had just seen you awake earlier that day; you were coming round. You were getting better. You weren't supposed to die. You were 48; you had no previous illnesses, no cancer, no diseases. How could this be? What happened? I will never forget the wee nurse apologising to us, saying they did everything they could. She also seemed shocked, and I believed her.

I did not sleep that night. I sat on the sofa all night and could not sleep. Everyone had gone to bed, but I stayed downstairs with my boyfriend whilst he fell asleep. I just sat in shock. I waited till the early morning to text my friend Jane. I asked to call her; she couldn't believe it and burst out crying, as did I, as the reality of actually saying it out loud hurt beyond all belief. The day was a blur after that, but I remember having to go back to the hotel we were booked into to get our stuff and check out. I remember the girl in reception went to my school, and I couldn't face her with my swollen face and eyeballs. On the way home, we stopped at Asda to get food or something to distract me, as I was just numb again. I bumped into someone I used to play handball with, and he was just staring at me and asked what had happened. This time, saying it face to face to someone hurt more. I just couldn't say it as he worriedly scanned my face. Jamie had to step in and tell him. He was a good family friend and loved my Mum, everyone did.

My Mum's brother was over from Ireland, and my aunt had come up from London; the house was starting to fill up. As an Irish Catholic family, a wake was very traditional for us. I saw my first dead body when I was 7 years old. My uncle John passed away when he was 42 from lung cancer. *(I believe he was the one who gave my Mum the salty milk when he came to take her.)* I remember coming down in the morning to my Mum wearing tea bags on her eyes to take the swelling down from crying.

This was something I should have done. My Dad and brother went to the funeral parlour to choose things like coffins, linings, flowers, and other things. It was quite overwhelming. Too much for my younger sisters. I was 21, and they were 19 and 17, and my brother was the oldest at 23. We decided to have a wake at the house in Scotland for two days. Then take her home to Ireland and bury her with her parents, as Ireland was home for all of us. Having a large Irish family, we had many wakes, and as a tradition for us, it felt right.

This wasn't a normal tradition in Scotland, but seeing the number of people turn up to the house to say goodbye to her was amazing and warmed my heart. I found it so comforting. The tradition is that the house is open for two days, day and night, and friends and family take it in turns to sit with the body, so they are never alone. After this, the priest comes to say the last prayer, and the coffin is carried by family to the hearse.

We started our first convoy to take the boat over to Ireland. There were about 20 family friends that came over with us. It made it quite exciting. We were met at Belfast dock by more family. They had driven the two hours to welcome their sister and auntie home. We then started our second convoy to her home, where she was taken to her brother's house, and the priest welcomed her into the house. This was the start of the second 2-day wake. This was a very different level, with more people, family, and friends. I remember there was a queue of people lined up to go in and see her, and I remember hugging everyone who was waiting to pay their last respects. I found it so amazing and comforting how many people came to show their final respects. My Mum was the youngest of 8 kids, and she was the second of the children to die, so it was a shock to the family. The two days of the wake passed in a blur. There were so many people, and we were all sharing a house with our friends who came over from Scotland. There were 20 of us in a house. I remember my sister slept on the floor of the dining room. We just all had to find a space, as it was such a small town and had no hotels.

On the second day was the funeral. The priest who carried out the sermon had never met my Mum, but he did a lot of research to explain her character by talking to many people about her. I appreciated how he described her. After that, a bat flew into the church and around the altar, which made everyone laugh and think that it was very typical of Kathleen to do such a thing. I agreed she had a great sense of humour and character and was often the life and soul of every room she walked into. She was bubbly and gregarious and connected easily with people. I was so proud to see how many lives she had touched. It was quite incredible. We lowered the coffin into the grave with her Mum and Dad; I had a corner, and my brother and other sisters had the other corners, and I started crying so hard I thought I was going to drop the rope. I think my brother Paul took all the strain at that moment. I was a mess. After four sleepless nights and many things going on, I broke.

Things after that were a blur. I only remember coming home to our house in Scotland after the whole thing, and our neighbours had prepared food and brought it over for us and welcomed us home, which I felt took the edge off coming home to a cold, empty house. That touched me. I thought it was such a caring and considerate thing to do. Things began to normalise and get back to reality. It had been a week of chaos and people. This is the part where the sadness and actual sense of what happened had time to set in. Trying to resume life again.

Our Dad had been living in Florida for the last few years; my parents were separated. Living with Dad again was weird. He also found it weird; he was used to his own space and life in a different country, and now he had to come back and sort things out. The weeks and months started to slip by, everyone trying to continue with their own lives. The change of season in the autumn and winter was hard for my Dad; he hated the cold. He felt he was not wanted and decided to sell the house; within three months, our childhood home was gone, and he moved back to the States. We all drifted apart in our hurt and pain. We couldn't help each other when we were all suffering. I decided to move to Ireland with Jamie. My brother was going to become a Dad for the first time; he knew before Mum died and didn't get to tell her. My sisters, I don't know where they were or how they were doing. We all splintered off.

I moved to Belfast with Jamie and tried to start a new life there. I thought being closer to where Mum was buried would help me feel less lost. I maintained close visits with her sisters and family, which brought comfort and a lesser sense of loss. It helped a little, I suppose, but didn't fill that hole. I filled the hole by eating. I became a comfort eater and put on about four stones over a few years. I threw myself into building a career. I had been at college studying graphic design, but I left and didn't finish when Mum became sick. I worked in retail and started working my way up, and after 8 years of living in Belfast and being with Jamie, I decided to move on and take a new opportunity. I had a great life in Belfast. We lived in a penthouse apartment in the centre, right on the riverfront, had a new car, and we both had great careers, but it wasn't making me happy. I had this urge to move to London, and I did with a work opportunity. Jamie had tried to come and transfer over, but it didn't work out for him, and we eventually broke up after 8 years together and a lot of traumas, as he lost his gran, who raised him, two years after I lost Mum. I think both of us having such losses young changed our paths.

London was mental; I worked 60 hours a week, was the skinniest I had ever been, and the loneliest. I moved into a shared house in Shepherd's Bush and met two new friends, an English guy named Dave and a South African called Sharon. Dave was sweet and caring, and Sharon was the bold, outgoing party animal. I liked the difference between them. We lived together for 5 years and had a lovely bond. They helped ground me in London. It's a vexatious city. My godparents also lived outside London, so I would often retreat to theirs for a weekend off to be fed and looked after, or have Christmas and holidays with them. Mary and Tony were always our closest family; maybe subconsciously that's why I decided to randomly move there. I fell in love with a guy from work; he was Spanish, and we were both tired of London. We wanted to travel so bought a motorhome and travelled Europe. I left some things with my aunt Mary and Tony, as I couldn't fit my whole life into a van.

We spent three months exploring Europe in a motorhome. Such freedom in having no plans and not living by the clock like you do in the UK or the corporate world.

We had agreed to move to Gibraltar and settle there, but it didn't feel right, so we moved to Alberto's hometown in Galicia, a beautiful remote part of Spain. I didn't speak a word of Spanish, but was optimistic I would learn quickly. We lived with his mother for nine months until I got a job. He was already working back at the family car dealership; that's why we moved back there; one of us was guaranteed a job. We got a flat eventually, and I tried to make it my space, but culturally it was so different for me. Language, food, customs, traditions, fiestas.

We travelled a lot to keep me inspired, as living in such a remote place after London was a big culture shock for me. We met an Australian guy who was also dating a Spaniard, and he tried to embrace the culture but struggled. They eventually moved back to Australia, but we visited them a few times, which was nice. They became great friends. My friend Sharon had moved to Mallorca with her family, and we went there often to visit. I enjoyed Mallorca a lot more; it was far more cosmopolitan than Ourense, and I didn't feel like an outsider so much. I eventually got to the stage where I became very sad and isolated after five years of trying to fit in, but you never do as a foreigner.

In 2017, I had been home three times for three funerals on my mother's side; one was my godmother, Mary. That had a huge impact on me. I realised life was too short to be unhappy, and I wasn't living there. I decided one morning that I wanted to move to Mallorca, much like I did the time I decided to move to London. I had been trying to teach English for five years and just wasn't very good at it, but I had learned to speak Spanish while trying to teach my own language, so at least something came from it.

I moved to Mallorca in August 2018, and Alberto and I broke up two months later. He couldn't leave his family business and hometown. I needed more. I had lost myself completely and needed to fill my soul again. I had become very sad and anxious. I moved over and stayed with Sharon and her family for 6 months whilst I got a job, my own flat, and settled on the island of my own accord. It was hard not knowing anyone or anything; I felt the most vulnerable I had in my entire life. I found it difficult to talk to people or look them in the eye. I didn't feel safe or whole. The friendship with Sharon, my best friend of 10 years, had broken down completely. We had changed and outgrown each other. My sister Natalie had moved over to stay with me, but that didn't work out.

We also fell out and weren't speaking, so in 2 years I had lost all the major people in my life. I was broken. I didn't know what was happening or where my life was going. I was alone for the first time in my life.

I met Linda through work and liked the fact she was Scottish. It felt familiar again. She helped me so much with work and life in general; she healed me. She listened to me whilst I tried to figure everything out; she helped me let go and flow. She also helped me look back and connect all my little dots. I always felt I ran away from things. But she helped me to look at things differently. Maybe I wasn't running away; maybe my lessons and time were done in situations. I was so scared of standing still and not doing something or going somewhere; it made me feel stuck or like I was wasting time. I wanted to fill my life with as much experience as possible. Life was a gift cut short for many.

I developed an irrational fear when I turned forty that as Mum died at forty-eight, I too would have only so long left. When Mary was diagnosed with lung cancer, I couldn't face seeing her not well. I was with her when she was diagnosed, but tried to distract her and convince her she would be fine. I couldn't give her the comfort she was looking for from me; she was scared, and that scared me. She died a month later, two months into her retirement. I didn't experience that with Mum, as she went so quickly. My Dad is now 72 and seeing him change and grow old is hard to watch, but I am trying to teach myself to find the grace in it; we are lucky to grow old.

When Mum died, my whole life flipped upside down and drastically changed on every level. I feared change after that and became sad and complacent. I didn't want anything to change ever again. What sort of life would that have been? Embracing change was the only option

I had to live my life. I learned to get excited about pushing myself in new challenges. I figured the worst thing that could happen had already happened, so I kept going forward, realising I could always go back physically. One thing I learned was that it was hard to go back mentally. Once you change and grow outside your hometown, it's very hard to move back. Going back to visit is familiar and comfortable for a time, but there's a yearning for more and achieving more.

I spent a long time trying to figure out what happened. *Why did she die?* It came out of nowhere. When people ask, they expect to hear about cancer or something tragic, but I never know what to say. I believe she gave up on life. Technically, her heart did give out, but there was no mention of heart trouble before, ever. She had become so unhappy in life; she was alone away from her family and had few friends in Scotland and became tired and lonely. We were all growing up and moving on, and she didn't want to be left alone; we were her life.

Life has taught me to look for the beauty in change. It forces us into the path we are supposed to be on, whether we like it or not. We're supposed to grow through the pain and fill our lives with the little things. The grief never changes, but as we grow and fill our lives with new friends that we truly connect with and not just grown-ups within the same school or town, the grief becomes less.

> **Grief and growth sometimes go hand in hand.**
>
> **You might mourn for what you've left behind even while you celebrate what you've gained.**

Let Them In

by Helen Lapierre

Grief is when your entire world falls apart and no one else's life changes
An experience like no other

Everything feels like it's crumbling around you while the rest of the world is moving forward...
as if nothing happened

Suddenly you're all alone in a roomful of people
My feelings of being alone overwhelmed me at times

Yet I was the one who isolated myself

When I did go out in the world, I felt as if I was trying to get on a moving merry go round
It's spinning faster and faster and I feared falling

*Grief is a natural part of life I learned it's ok to take the time you need
There is no right or wrong*

*We are not alone
You are not alone
There are people who do care and want to support you*
Let them in

*I took that leap onto the merry go round
I fell...
But there were others around me who picked me up
I fell less and less with the help of loving hands sent from Heaven*

Until we meet again...

Helen Lapierre, Mom & Founder of Hello to Heaven

https://www.hellotoheaven.com

The Gift in Grief

Linda Ledwidge

The Gift in Grief

Grief breaks the ground beneath my feet,

Yet in that darkness, new roots appear.

A seed of self begins to grow—

From the pain, deep sorrow I sow.

Not just the loss, not just the ache,

But a strength I didn't know it could wake.

The slender cracks let in the light—

And shape my soul more clear, more bright.

This is the gift: not just to be,

But to grow into a new, brave me.

"Embrace your grief. For there, your soul will grow."
~Carl Jung~

Grief Reveals Us

by Ayelet Baron

No one prepares us for grief, apart from life itself, when we face endings head-on.

Although our education system equips us with various skills and knowledge, it rarely openly talks about how to navigate one of the most universal human experiences—grief. This is where reality deepens. We exist to experience the full spectrum of life, from sadness to joy, without suppressing our feelings.

Humanity stands at a pivotal point where much is being revealed, and our reactions are our own choice. As part of nature, we recognise that everything has a beginning and an end. Life and death are integral to our existence.

Can we consider grief as a means to appreciate what matters to us and to cherish each moment? The present moment, like this very night, will never recur. Grief, following the initial shock and healing from an ending, offers us a front-row seat to life's unfolding mystery.

Samantha Hunt, in *"The Unwritten Book,"* reflects on endings—humans, winters, childhoods, love affairs, and books. Their endings are sharp, painful, yet rich with meaning, revealing the true work of our bodies: to feel deeply.

From a young age, death has been a part of my life. My earliest memory is of war breaking out when I was three years old, witnessing communities unite against a common enemy. War invariably brings loss of life, and it explained the small size of my family as I grew older. Gathered with my neighbours in the bomb shelter, we listened anxiously to the radio while uniformed officers arrived to deliver news of loved ones lost. This wasn't a scene from a movie; it was the harsh reality of life. It took time, but I came to realise that if my *"side"* had lost, you wouldn't be reading these words now. The enemy's objective was to erase everything I stood for, including me, from the planet.

This understanding led me to realise that humans create conflict, war, and division. From a young age, I actively sought to heal these divides, later recognising that I could only contribute my part.

The Native American grandmothers would ask their grandchildren, *"Do you want to attract miracles into your life? Do your part."*

"You have no responsibility to save the world or find the solutions to all problems—but to attend to your particular personal corner of the universe. As each person does that, the world saves itself. We each can make a world of difference."

Today, many are feeling the impact of decisions made by loved ones choosing to depart this world. We seek to understand and openly discuss these choices, emphasising the importance of talking openly about anything and everything. We can never fully know what others face.

Losing someone we love shatters our world, creating an emptiness hard to comprehend. Grieving is one of the most genuine human experiences we engage in. Each of us faces our own set of circumstances, characterised by loss, grief, and sadness, both individually and collectively.

In my mid-20s, I faced a profound loss. A close person tried to reach me at work, but I was too busy to answer. I planned to return the call later, but that opportunity never came. For years, guilt and regret haunted me. This loss, however, also turned into a gift. It taught me that we only have this moment. Work is part of life, not its purpose. I vowed to help myself and others understand that we cannot equate our self-worth with what we do for a living.

Maybe an opportunity to ask children, *"What do you love?" "What lights you up?"* Instead of *"What do you want to be?"*

Years later, a journey with 18 women to the Amazon Rainforest introduced me to the Achuar tribe, who view death simply as part of life's natural cycle. In the Amazon, I realised we are not separate from nature, but an integral part of it. Understanding natural cycles helps us grasp that change is natural, not something to manage.

In the stillness of an Amazon night, by the river, surrounded by the sounds of birds and water, I had a profound conversation with the person I had lost suddenly. There, I forgave him for leaving and forgave myself as well. I had often thought things might have been different if I had taken the call. Yet, I hadn't, and all I could do was learn to flow with what life presented.

Natural cycles teach us about life and death. A tree in a garden sees more in its lifetime than a human ever will. While we might think we own land or trees, in the end, nature has the final say—vegetation ultimately consumes us. The only true certainty in life is death; everything else—our stories, structures, and systems—is man-made creations or inheritances.

Many Indigenous cultures believe in continuation rather than an end. No one truly knows what lies beyond, only beliefs and stories shared by those who have had near-death experiences.

During transitions, people enter and leave our lives. Life and death are natural cycles, and happiness is only part of the human experience. ***Grief is an expression of profound love.***

When in harmony with ourselves, we manage emotions without extreme highs and lows because we are attuned to life's natural flow. We learn to acknowledge endings, grieve in our way, and appreciate the fleeting nature of our existence. Those who have passed remain with us, encouraging and loving us from beyond.

Facing death helps us come alive, recognising that aging is natural and that societal narratives often paint an incomplete picture.

Grief is both a personal and a collective experience. As we face global challenges and personal losses, our collective grieving process can lead to a deeper understanding and a shared path forward.

Living with awareness of impermanence transforms our approach to life, urging us to live more authentically and make choices reflecting our deepest values.

Grief reveals our values, capacity for love, and resilience. By embracing grief, we open ourselves to a fuller experience of life, recognising that each ending also heralds a new beginning.

Not everyone comes with us as we make conscious choices about who is healthy and toxic for our own well-being. Not everyone is, and that's okay. With eight billion people on the planet, there is abundance. And yet, when we walk away from toxic situations, we also grieve the loss and also the realisation that there were beginnings patiently waiting for us to get out of our own way.

What are your grief experiences? How do they shape your life?. What if we viewed every loss not just as an end but as an invitation to a richer, more engaged life?

Here's to feeling deeply, speaking openly about our feelings, grieving our losses, and healing at our own pace.

This tidal wave, when we let it break our hearts open, may cleanse us, preparing us for the new world and the new selves we are becoming. Not everyone will join us, as each of us authors our own story and makes our own choices.

Tara Branch, in her book *"True Refuge,"* notes that in the Lakota/Sioux tradition, those grieving are considered most holy. Grief opens us to the groundless openness of sorrow, a wholeness of presence, and a deep natural wisdom.

Everyone grieves differently. Many fear death, yet it is an integral part of our journey. We each have the opportunity to live fully right now, making choices that reflect our true selves without apology.

We've been taught to deeply fear death, but life and death are part of our trek. So many try to stay youthful, and yet, aging is a natural process that we've been conditioned to suppress. When we truly face the fact that one day everything dies, including us, a new desire may spring within us to actually come alive.

I know many inspirational individuals who are no longer physically here and who taught me to live fully. I remember a final conversation, filled with laughter, with someone who left way too early. A reminder that the certainty of outcomes never truly comes.

How we show up for ourselves and each other matters, and maybe we reflect on what becomes possible when we choose to be powerful creators? What are we living for?

We learn to become aware and feel deeply into endings and grieve in our own way.

We can also realise how fleeting this life we have been truly gifted is and know whoever left the physical world is still with us, cheering us on and loving us.

If you too are grieving, I send warm embraces and a dose of peace.

The tears never stop for me, but they plant seeds of creation.

♡

YOU are OK

It's OK to be OK,
and
It's OK not to be OK,
and
It's OK to be OK again.
Each time, it changes.
It's OK

YOU are OK

Grief and Loss

by Amanda J Butler

I awoke in the middle of the night and burst into tears. I didn't know why—I couldn't explain it. Had I been dreaming? I pondered, as I heard a deep, mournful sob escape my lips. I didn't think so. I became aware of a deep sorrow that seemed to be coming from the depths of my soul. *What on earth is wrong with you?* I asked myself, trying to hold back my emotion. I felt my whole body trembling; my breath came in ragged gasps as I desperately fought to hold back the tears.

But to no avail; I started sobbing uncontrollably, and a mournful, low-pitched wail escaped my lips. *"What on earth is wrong with you, Amanda?"* my boyfriend asked me, rather astounded at my behaviour. We'd just had a really fun night and had no idea what had set me off.

"I don't know," I gasped in between sobs, *"It's like I've lost someone."* As the sobs overwhelmed me, my breaths came in quick, shallow gasps, each inhalation a desperate attempt to find air amid the waves of emotion. My chest tightened - my heart raced against my ribcage, leaving me dizzy and disorientated, caught in a cycle of gasping and weeping that seemed to stretch time itself. I eventually calmed myself down and, rather bewildered, fell into an exhausted sleep. I'd never behaved like that before - he must have thought I'd gone mad.

It was a cool autumn Friday night, September 21st, 1990. My boyfriend at the time was an officer in the RAF, living on an RAF base on the outskirts of London. As part of their social calendar, the officers had organised an 'Oktoberfest' in the Officers' Mess with several friends and other Officers, all dressed in Lederhosen or German-style 'Hansel and Gretel' outfits. Everyone had enjoyed a fun-themed dinner, drank Weiss Beer, and sang Oom-Pa-Pa like Baron Bomburst in Chitty Chitty Bang Bang. We were all staying overnight in the Mess, with eight other friends, and very merrily wished each other good night. It had been such a fun evening. I fell asleep as soon as my head hit the pillow. The next thing I knew, I was crying my eyes out for no apparent reason, which was so not me.

The following morning, I slowly came to, feeling rather fragile. My eyes still closed, I started to recall the events of the night before and wondered if perhaps I'd had a bad dream. But no, to my body, it felt raw and very real, whatever it was. It wasn't a dream. I hadn't drunk that much, so it wasn't a drunken outburst. I checked myself, feeling quite exhausted having cried myself to sleep. Chris was still asleep.

I rose quietly and went to the bathroom to wash my face, wondering what on earth had possessed me the night before. I stared at myself in the mirror; my eyes looked puffy. Hmm, how odd - I was still feeling very out of sorts and couldn't understand why.

The next thing I knew, there was a knock on the bedroom door in the Officers' quarters - *"Morning, Sir, sorry to disturb you, but there's a phone call for Amanda"*, the voice said. *"Oh God,"* I said, with a feeling of foreboding. It was a time before most people had mobile phones, but I had told my parents where I would be; it had been planned for some time. I pulled some clothes on as if in a heavy fog, my heart pounding. A cold sweat covered my brow as I walked slowly down the corridor to the phone, time stretching around me as if everything was moving in slow motion.

"Hello," I said apprehensively. There was a sharp intake of breath on the other end of the line. *"Hello, Amanda, it's Dad."*

"Yes," I said with a long pause......" *What's wrong?"* I asked, a dreaded inner knowing pressing heavily on my heart.

"It's Simon." Another long pause. *"He's had an accident."* My brother was away on business in Israel. *"Paragliding."* I caught my breath.

"So, what does that mean? Is he in the hospital? What have they said?" I said anxiously, thinking perhaps he was in the hospital with multiple broken bones. Silence, another catch of breath at the other end. *"Dad......?!!!"* My hand started shaking; I felt as if I was going to be sick.

I heard his fractured words, with my mother's surprisingly muted crying in the background.

I heard this strange sound in my ears. It was a sound of such deep sorrow and pain, strangely reminiscent of last night, I reflected.... I then realised that the deep basal cry was coming from me, echoing the sound I'd made in the night.

My dearest brother, Simon, was three years older than I (27). My best friend, my closest sibling, my mentor, and my ally was gone. My life as I knew it was to be irrevocably changed.

Chris came over to try to comfort me, along with my other rather anxious and concerned friends who had stayed overnight. Time seemed to be running in painful slow motion; it was all so surreal. I returned to my room, clearly in shock, packing up my overnight case with shaking hands in a complete daze. *"No, not Simon. Not my Simon!! It can't be. I don't believe it,"* my mind exploded. I just couldn't comprehend it.

The next few days passed by as if I were stuck in a thick fog. We were informed that Simon had died instantly from the fatal impact of his paraglider slamming against a cliff. He often went out flying after work and had taken his paraglider with him to Israel whilst on business. He had been 'picked up' by a thermal during a late afternoon flight, but the wind had suddenly changed direction, and turbulence had thrust him into the cliff face at high speed. He had probably been focused on trying to reopen his chute - and then the forceful impact.; immediate, no time for pain. All over in an instant, or so we prayed.

I reflected on that night so many times over the years. So strange that somehow, through the ether, I knew he had passed. Had my reaction been a strange premonition, or were our souls connected? I didn't know the definitive answer, but there was no doubt in my mind that we are not just flesh and blood, and there must be something more in the afterlife. We'd had a strong connection, in contact nearly every day, unless he was away on business. He'd been my best friend, my everything. I had been so proud to call him my brother. He had been so talented and excelled at everything he seemed to touch. Everyone was drawn to him, like a moth to a flame. I absolutely adored him.

We subsequently found out Simon had been out flying by himself, trying out his new paraglider. He'd arranged to meet one of his new clients for dinner that evening, but he hadn't turned up. His client had thought it strange, but it was only later that night when he had heard of a paragliding accident with a foreigner on the radio that he contacted the police. His company had notified the local police, who arrived at my parents' door at dawn the next day. Knowing I was going to a party, they had delayed telling me for another day, trying to keep the devastating news from me for a few remaining hours of my innocent bliss. Before my heart was ripped open and my life was turned upside down. Oh God, Simon… how could you leave me?

It was a Sliding Doors moment—up until that moment in time, my life had been very blessed. A close-knit family, loving and supportive parents. Our childhood had been mostly carefree, filled with the magic of an expatriate lifestyle. We weren't wealthy in the traditional sense, but my father's salary was offset with a life rich in five-star travel, beautiful homes in exotic places with staff, and a childhood overflowing with boisterous, carefree fun, laughter, and exciting adventures. Fast-forward to 1990—my parents were now retired and settled in England, and destiny had cast its die. In an instant, our lives had shattered, splintering into unrecognisable pieces.

At six years old, I recall being told that my grandparents—on my father's side—had passed away. I was saddened, of course, but only for a night or so; we hadn't spent much time with them, having lived abroad. A few years later, my best friend died, which felt tragic, but we hadn't seen each other in over a year since returning from my father's posting in Alaska. I had again been very sad at the time, but I was still so young. But losing a close sibling, and my soulmate, was something else entirely.

Coming from a family of five children, with three older brothers and a twin brother, it was unusual for a brother three years my senior to be my closest sibling. But girls generally mature much earlier than boys, and when we were younger, I had much more in common with Simon than with my twin. He had always been the shining light in any room. Humorous, charismatic, and dynamic, he was the glue that held all of us siblings together, bridging the large age gap of ten years between the eldest and youngest.

We'd all been placed in boarding school whilst my parents were travelling the globe for my father's work with British Airways. Simon would often come and visit me at my school. He was so debonair and self-assured, good-looking, and generally pretty 'cool', as many of my girlfriends had reflected with their coquettish reactions. I recall asking him to promise that he'd never leave me, which, in retrospect, was a strange thing to say. (I have often wondered whether my soul had known, in some way, what was to come.) Simon's death was my first true introduction to the brutal reality of loss.

The days that followed unfolded in a surreal form of disbelief. I went through the motions as if viewing from afar much of the time. But then, occasionally, feelings of complete and utter devastation would suddenly envelop me - I would leave the room as inconspicuously as possible, going to the privacy of my bedroom to just crumble and cry uncontrollably. Once I regained my composure, I would return downstairs to try to be as much of a support to my mother as possible, although much of the time she was lost in her own desolate solitude.

Simon's company was very kind to us. They took care of everything and were incredibly generous, considering he had only been with them for six months. They offered to take the whole family to Tel Aviv to bring Simon home. My parents, my second eldest brother Michael, my twin brother Oliver, and I were all to make the tragic journey to collect him and return his body to his home in Buckinghamshire.

Simon's senior director, John, was designated to accompany us. He was a nice, gentle, cuddly bear of a man — very kind, sympathetic, and incredibly stoic, considering the very difficult job ahead of him. My mother was a bereaved mess. They booked us into the Hilton Hotel in Tel Aviv, where Simon had been staying. His room was cordoned off, with his belongings just as he had left them, heading out to enjoy what were to be his final moments, 'soaring with the eagles' as my father subsequently added to his epitaph – *Dying as he had lived, soaring with the eagles.'* Always flying by the seat of his pants with so much energy, passion, and drive - the centre of attention in any room. The centre of attention in my life, that was for sure.

I adored and admired him. He was my mentor - he inspired me, guided me into my career in the hotel industry (since I didn't really know what I wanted to do), and like all of us, loved to travel. A friend of his had taken a degree in hotel management, and he advised me that it could lead to any career I wanted, particularly travel, a passion we shared. He was always doing something new and exciting, making me laugh, making everyone laugh, and he was the brother with whom I had most in common. He was my best friend, my life, and I was broken. We were all broken.

We were invited to pay our last respects at the morgue. My mother and father went in first - Mum leaving a devastated wreck, with my father having to support her when leaving the room. Then it was my turn. I chose to go in by myself, to have our last moment together. I gulped and held my breath as I entered.

There he was, lying on a cold marble slab, dressed in his office suit. How bizarre. Surely, I'm going to wake up and realise this is just a hideous nightmare? I looked down at him, observing—curiously detached. His face was covered in an unnatural layer of orange-toned makeup, his hair slicked back. They must have gone to his hotel room and chosen his final outfit—an office suit. I nearly wretched. But I didn't cry. I studied him more closely, searching for something familiar - yet he felt like a stranger. This wasn't Simon. My dearest brother was no longer there. What lay before me was merely a vessel—stiff, cold, lifeless—preserved for five days, waiting for us to arrive. They had done their best to make him presentable, despite the trauma of the impact. Surprisingly, he looked intact, with no visible facial injuries. But he was different. Hard, cold, soulless, with the ridiculously awful makeup and the stiff business suit - it was all so wrong. No smile, no naughty twinkle in his eye. Oh my God, it just wasn't him. Simon was gone. In that moment, I knew, with absolute certainty, that there was so much more to life - and death.

We had been brought up in a Christian household. My parents had met and married overseas in Hong Kong. With my father working for British Airways, they had made their friends wherever they were stationed, predominantly based around the internationally familiar Anglican Church congregation. They were always welcoming and engaging - an immediate ready-made 'family' in any new country. Having been born in Egypt and living amongst both Muslims and Christians, I realised on reflection that I had always been more spiritual than religious, seeing more similarities between faiths rather than division. Yes, I believed in a higher power– God, Yahweh, Source, the Divine, whatever one chooses to call He, She, or It. But from the day my brother had died, my mother declared she did not. How could a God allow this to happen, for him to abandon her? She was so very angry. My father, on the other hand, was always of the notion that she (and we) should be grateful for what we had, rather than what we didn't. His positive attitude at this time was not overly welcomed by my very devastated, grieving mother.

So where was Simon? Where did he go? His body was now just a hollow vessel, his soul departed. But where? I asked the Heavens. *"Why did you have to go, Simon? Why did you leave me?"* I shouted out into the troubled depths of my mind. We were all feeling rather broken, numb, just empty.

We returned to the Hilton hotel and sat in the lobby, attempting to make polite conversation with Simon's manager, John. He'd had to help my father support my mother back to the hotel, in a very sorry state. Tea was ordered in the lobby. The piano started playing as we stared into space, stuck in our own version of the Twilight Zone (which had been a supernatural series we'd enjoyed as young children).

Oliver was seated beside me. Being the same age, we had something of a love-hate relationship at the time. But Simon's demise had united us in our grief. I turned to Oliver and murmured, *"Oli, go ask the pianist to play Simon's songs"*. Simon was multi-talented and quite a gifted pianist. His renditions had been quite diverse, but he had a certain few he had loved playing with great gusto - Für Elise, Crocodile Pock, and Romeo and Juliet. Not exactly a similar genre.

My attention drifted off. But my focus returned to the room as the tinkling notes of Für Elise filtered through my consciousness. I glanced at Oliver. I hadn't seen him rise. The song finished, and Romeo and Juliet followed straight afterward. I looked up. *"Oli, I didn't see you get up - did you speak with the pianist?"* I questioned. *"No, I thought you had?"* he said questioningly, and we both looked at each other in surprise. A few more tunes played, and then the lead-in notes to Crocodile Rock began to play. Tears welled up in our eyes. *"Oli, he's here. He's with us. He's trying to tell us* he's ok.*"* I looked at Oliver in amazement. Wow, what were the odds of that happening? I pondered. We didn't say anything to Mum, she was just too incoherent in her despair.

That night, I chose to have a spare bed made up in my parents' room, rather than sleep in a room by myself. My parents had the bed made up under the window. I wished them both good night in a hushed monotone; we were all shell-shocked, hardly speaking. I fell asleep.

My whole being spent.

I stirred - something had brought me out of a deep sleep. I turned over, caught between sleep and semi-consciousness. It was still dark; I was still half asleep, but then I sensed a comforting hand very gently touching mine. A feeling of such love seemed to emanate from this gentle touch - such a soothing gesture, making me feel like a child being comforted back to sleep. How thoughtful of Mum to be thinking of me, despite her own sorrow, I thought, as I fell back to sleep.

In the morning, I awoke with the light filtering through from beneath the heavy hotel curtains. I opened my eyes, slightly disoriented. Recalling the night before, I glanced over to my mother and noticed I was more than an arm's length away from Mum's side of the bed she shared with my father. I wondered to myself how she would have been able to reach me in the night without getting up, since I hadn't heard her get up. It had felt like a gentle yet firm hand. Had I dreamt it? No - it had felt so real, and I had taken great comfort from it.

"Mum," I said, *"did you get up in the night and put your hand on me?"* I asked.

"No, it wasn't me, Manda," she said quietly, lost in her painful thoughts. I looked at my father - he shook his head.

"Hmm, ok." I pondered. Again, another sign from my brother, *"I haven't left you, Amanda, I'm here".*

Returning with him to the UK, saying our last goodbyes at the funeral, breaking down by the graveside as I watched his coffin being lowered into the freshly dug dark hole in the ground...... it was all a hideous blur. I went through the motions. A slow and painful process.

After this initial period of shock, the grieving process began. Denial, anger, despair. Then depression. I noticed how odd it was that people I knew well didn't even mention him or even look me in the eye. It felt like they were even avoiding me. Many were, of course, scared to say anything to add to the upset, with the customary awkwardness that so often comes with not knowing how to deal with such a tragic loss of one so young. I became quite upset, feeling my so-called 'friends' didn't seem to care. I was also doing my best to console my mother, but she was so angry at the world, at God, at life, at my father - at anyone and everything. She was inconsolable.

It was unfortunate that I had been just two weeks into my first London job, having recently returned from a gap year (or two in my case) in Australia. My first job in the corporate world was in hotel sales, and I had just completed my sales training course when the atom bomb exploded. I returned to my new job at the Selfridge Hotel in London two weeks later, several kilos lighter, with the light in my eyes much diminished. It was difficult to concentrate, but I tried to stay focused on my new job. I guess it was something new to take my mind off my broken heart. I just about managed but would take the tube back to my apartment in Southfields, staring into the void (or so it felt), holding in my grief in public spaces as best I could. When at home alone, with my attention not taken up by a new job or people around me, waves of emotion would hit me with the force of a stormy sea, when I would least expect it. It would take me up in its powerful surge, tumbling me through the memories and sorrow, leaving me breathless and exhausted in its wake. Racing thoughts, sleepless nights, chaotic, negative chatter of fear and loss. And then I would have to rise again, into a world that didn't understand what I was going through. I had lost my brother!!! He was never coming back!

I got through it, somehow. But it changed me, it changed us - and it changed our family dynamic forever. My grandmother on my mother's side passed away four months later. She'd suffered a stroke shortly after Simon's passing. Mum had not recovered and could be quite difficult to be around, being so forlorn and sad most of the time. My three other brothers came home less frequently, and we certainly never had our normal big family Christmas and any other family gatherings we had been used to.

She carried on with life but was a changed woman, crying a great deal that first year. Her tears lessened. Of course, she loved us all - and me in particular, as her only daughter - but she had lost her zest for life. Her anger turned into fear of anything any of us might do that could be deemed dangerous. (She would have had an apoplectic fit if she'd known I had contemplated continuing to paraglide, which was a promise I'd made to Simon before his death, oddly enough. I decided against it, although Oliver and Michael carried on a short while after.) Although never diagnosed as such, my mother was obviously in depression. She focused most of her attention on me and would move through cycles of paranoia that one of us would also die. She never accepted Simon's loss.

The rest of the family carried on, each of us navigating our way through grief in our own way. My eldest brother Adrian, already more inclined toward faith than the rest of us, found solace in his Church, becoming an even more devout believer. My second eldest brother, Michael, whose last conversation with Simon had been an argument—there had been a fair amount of competition between them—became quite bitter and withdrawn. Though he never spoke of it, the weight of those last words clearly haunted him, and he became more distant. For my twin brother and me, however, the tragedy had the opposite effect—it drew us closer. And in the midst of so much loss, that was the one good thing we could hold on to.

I spent the rest of the year and more, going through what I now realise is part of the Five Stages of Grief – from disbelief to anger and despair, bargaining, moments of depression, to a very slow, reluctant acceptance.

I was fortunate in some ways, difficult as it was, in having to focus on my new career. I had also started spending more time with my new boyfriend, who had briefly met Simon before he died. He also came from a large family, the opposite of mine, with four sisters. It felt very important to me that Richard had met Simon; it helped. Although I was always there for my mother, I preferred spending time with Richard's family, finding 'fun' elsewhere. I relished the escapism of being part of a 'complete' and loving family unit again.

My grief eased slowly, year by year. I would say I never got over it, I just got on with it. Distractions helped immensely, as did friends with whom I could reminisce when my grief got the better of me. All of it lessened with the passage of time - the greatest of healers, cleanly expressed in the Persian proverb,' This Too Shall Pass'.

My mother, however, never got over the loss of her Golden Child. Ten years after Simon's death, she was diagnosed with a brain tumour, something which I sincerely believe was brought about by her unrelinquished grief. We were to experience grief from quite a different perspective over a much longer period. It had taken two years of dizzy symptoms, sweats, nausea, and a multitude of tests for her 'post-menopausal symptoms' to be finally diagnosed with a brain tumour. We nearly lost her mid-operation, but she came back around. She was 65, quite young in relative terms. She had tried to get on with normal life as best she could, supporting the church and the Town's Women's Guild, keeping her busy. My dad would often remind her how fortunate she was to have three other sons and a 'beautiful daughter'. Mum would get angry with him and say, *'That's not the point'* - she didn't believe in any God anymore. *"Why would a loving God take my son away from me?"* She was a wounded soul, with the light in her eyes rarely to be seen, apart from the occasional fleeting moments, which were few and far between.

I had been fortunate to be able to start working from home amid all this. I had been blessed with a wonderful client with whom I'd established a close relationship. Having lost her own mother, she very kindly offered to give me her business exclusively when she heard the news. It would enable me to work from home, organising her department's conferences and incentives, in which I now specialised. So, I rented out my apartment in Wimbledon and moved into my parents' house in Derbyshire to help my father look after my mother.

This time, the grief process was very different. Her illness was a slow, debilitating decline. I fought with the oncologist, who immediately wanted to tell my mother that his prognosis was three to six months at best - if she was lucky. I put my foot down. *"Absolutely not".* She was very easily influenced, and if she knew, we were sure she would go downhill rapidly. He very reluctantly said nothing. We wanted to give her some form of hope, so I decided we would try some alternative therapies to try to alleviate the harsh effects that radio and chemotherapy were having on her poor, frail body.

I suggested we try every alternative therapy I could find in the Yellow Pages (the only business telephone directory available at the time). Reiki, Acupuncture, Hands-On spiritual healing - you name it, we tried it. I would expound upon my wonderful experience, even if I felt nothing. We exceeded the oncologist's six-month 'sell-by' date considerably, and she was doing quite well, considering.

I remember a poignant moment with my mother, helping her bathe when she became much less able. As I gently washed her frail body, she murmured, *"You're so gentle, like you're washing a baby."* Then, with a soft, wistful chuckle, she added, *"You'll make a wonderful mother one day."* Her words, so tender yet laced with sadness, tightened something deep in my heart. It felt surreal—this was my mother, once so strong, now so vulnerable. My heart ached for her, for the dignity she had lost, for the pain she bore so bravely. I swallowed hard, holding back my tears.

But 14 months on, she began to decline once again. Her headaches were getting worse, and her agitation and impatience became more pronounced. The tumour had returned. We were given *Sophie's choice* by her surgeon, as the cancer was rapidly advancing again. She could have another operation, or there was also a new cancer trial for which she might qualify. Whatever the decision, the look of both concern and empathy in the surgeon's eye just seemed like we would merely prolong the inevitable. The operation had been so traumatic for her, and she was now so frail. We didn't feel she was strong enough for it, so we prayed for a miracle from this new clinical trial. This appeared to have some positive effects, as her energy picked up and she became more alert. But we still knew, deep down, it was just a matter of time.

I was then offered a far too tempting sailing holiday to accompany my boyfriend Richard on a yacht delivery with a captain friend of his. I'd been helping to care for my mother for 18 months. It had all taken its toll on me emotionally and physically, so naturally, my father encouraged me to go, as did she. I felt I just needed a break, and this was such a once-in-a-lifetime opportunity - three weeks on a private yacht! I was easily persuaded, albeit with a mixed feeling of excitement tinged with guilt. My brothers would be there to take turns to help support my dad.

So, off I went on a private 150-foot motor yacht from Phuket to Bali with a group of seven people - four of whom I knew. I kept in touch by phone as much as the variable connectivity allowed, which wasn't very frequent in those days. Mum seemed pretty good in general. But two weeks into the voyage, she became paranoid about me being eaten by sharks. Not a good sign.

What I hadn't realised was that, without my persistent protection, my mother's oncologist had finally prevailed. Eighteen months after his initial prognosis of "six months at best," he told her she had only weeks left. Whether it was a coincidence or not, within two weeks, she was in serious decline. My father broke the news to me, but my brothers reassured me, *"Finish your holiday as planned,"* they said. *"You'll be back in a week, and there are going to be rough times ahead. Enjoy these last few days, Amanda."*

It would have been difficult to return sooner anyway, but part of me clung to their words—any excuse to delay the inevitable. Lost in the magic of this surreal voyage, I let myself drift for just a little longer. But now, it was time to go home.

On arrival in the UK, I had a brief one-day stopover planned in Wales with my partner to attend a wedding before returning home to my parents. As soon as I arrived, I called home - my father put my mother on the phone, *"Manda,"* a long-laboured pause, *"you're home safe. Thank heavens". "Yes, Mum, I'm back. I've missed you so much; I'll be home with you tomorrow."* Little did I know these were the last words I was to hear from my mother. It was as if she had been waiting for my return. She had needed to know I was safely home before she finally surrendered; a few hours later, she sank into a semi-comatose state. I left for home immediately.

I won't describe the next ten days in full detail, but it passed in a heavy, sorrowful blur – I found myself back in the Twilight Zone. My dearest mother was home under palliative care, hooked up to morphine with a drip and catheter, lying mostly unconscious in a hospital bed in the lounge. My twin brother and father were there, and we took turns to be with her, holding her hand, stroking her forehead, and keeping her mouth hydrated with a swab we dipped in water. I sometimes slept beside her since the bed was quite wide, reading stories to her late into the night.

Her eyes remained closed most of the time, but occasionally, they would flicker open, filled with alarm—pleading, searching, trying to communicate but unable to speak. We soon realised this happened whenever her catheter was blocked, causing her clear discomfort. The visiting nurse repeatedly reassured us that nothing was wrong, only to be proven otherwise time and again. It was difficult to blame her for her detached demeanour, but the whole situation was deeply upsetting.

After what felt like ten endless days, my mother grew weaker. I had once read that, in end-of-life moments, gently letting a loved one know it's okay to go, and that those they are leaving behind will be ok, can help them find the peace to be able to move on.

"Mummy, I think it's time for you to go. You've been through enough. We'll all be fine, and I promise we'll take care of Dad for you. Follow

the light—go to Simon, he's waiting for you. We love you so much. Thank you for being such a wonderful, loving mother," I whispered, pressing a gentle kiss to her cheek as tears streamed down my face. The sorrow was overwhelming—this was my dear, sweet mother, and what a cruel fate she had endured. I silently prayed for her suffering to end quickly. I stayed by her side a little longer until my brother Oliver came to take over. I popped upstairs for a shower, wondering if today would be our final goodbye.

As I came out of the shower, I heard Oliver shout. *"Come quick, I think she's going."* By the time my father and I ran downstairs to her, her breathing had just stopped, and her body was limp. She was finally at peace. *"Goodbye, Mummy. We all loved you so much. Go to Simon; he's waiting for you."* I said out loud. We embraced one another in our shared sorrow. She was finally out of her pain and misery; thank heavens.

Even more surreal—and with painfully imperfect timing—my brother Adrian's wedding was on that very same day; that was the reason he wasn't with us. It had been decided that Michael would go in our stead, representing the family. But now we had a choice, which at that moment felt like a script in a black comedy.

Dazed and grieving, we had to decide. After a brief discussion, we decided that Mum had chosen to leave this earthly plane at this moment, so we could all be there for Adrian. But could we really find the strength to attend a wedding just hours after losing her? And then, the unspoken reality: we would have to carry on as if nothing had happened; leaving her still-warm body behind in the living room, stepping into a celebration while our hearts ached with her loss. Yet somehow, it did seem to be our dear mother's dying wish.

So, we collectively took a deep breath, made the calls we needed to make, and gathered ourselves as quickly as possible with all our wedding clothes, leaving her not-yet-cold body in the middle of the lounge. The vicar had said he would sort everything out so we could go - how kind.

As we left, my father handed me Mum's wedding and engagement rings – *"She would have wanted you to have them, Love",* he said. I hesitated, feeling it wasn't quite right, but looking up into my Father's watery eyes, I slipped them both onto my right-hand ring finger. *"Oh God Mum – how very surreal this all is,"* I thought, tears running down my cheeks.

We each said our last goodbyes, picked up our overnight bags, and walked out the door. I looked back for the last time at her now peaceful body, took a deep breath, and closed the door behind me – *Goodbye Mum.*

We had just enough time to make the five-hour drive to get to the church in Saint Davids, West Wales, which felt like it couldn't have been designed to be further away if you'd tried. My poor father was very quiet. Mum was 13 years younger than he; this was not what he had expected. But he was strong and incredibly resilient, resigned to the task ahead.

I called Adrian from the car, who had already been informed of Mum's passing. *"Adrian, we've decided to brave it and come to the wedding; it was clearly Mum's wish for us to be with you as a family. Please tell Carys not to tell any of the guests about Mum; we don't want to detract from your special day. We'll be ok; just please make sure we're all sat together. We haven't got the energy for small talk."*

We made it to the church just 15 minutes late, which was a bit of a miracle as it was. *"You're late, we've all been waiting for you to start!"* Carys' mother muttered to me in annoyance, as we tried to slip quietly into the front pew as inconspicuously as possible - the whole congregation watching the three of us file in alongside Michael. Oh God, what a surreal nightmare of a day - it was going to take all the strength we had to get through this.

I closed my eyes and tried to regain my composure as the service began, Adrian and Carys focusing on their special day, beaming from ear to ear. Poor Dad - he put such an incredibly brave face on, having just lost his dear beloved wife of 46 years that very same morning. It was certainly a wedding we would remember, but sadly for all the wrong reasons.

This time, my grief felt very different. We had already endured the sudden, devastating loss of my brother at far too young an age—a tragedy that had shattered us. But with my mother, the sorrow had been unfolding for months, even years. We had been grieving for her long before she was gone, watching helplessly as she faded—losing her faculties, her dignity, and eventually, herself. By the time she took her final breath, there was a quiet relief alongside the sadness. No more pain. No more suffering. It is said that losing a child is the most unbearable grief a mother can endure. My beloved mother carried that sorrow with her until the very end—mourning her son with every breath, until her very last breath was spent.

Four months later, in September 2002, I moved to the island of Mallorca with my partner Richard—a plan set in motion two years before, just before my mother's diagnosis. After the emotional toll of the past two years, I was ready to reset, to begin anew, and to heal. Mallorca welcomed me in a gentle embrace, offering a way of life and its breathtaking landscapes that helped nourish my soul. I was fortunate to cross paths with incredible healers and therapists, each helping me unravel the layers of pain that had settled deep within me. I needed healing—mind, body, and spirit—and there was no better place to find it. And so, a new chapter began.

I had made a promise—to myself and my mother's memory—that I would find a way to help others facing cancer. I wasn't yet sure how, but after witnessing the devastating side effects of chemotherapy and radiation, I began researching holistic cancer treatments. With the Internet now at my fingertips, I delved into alternative approaches to healing.

I started compiling an information email to share with anyone newly diagnosed, offering guidance on holistic steps to support their journey—how to adjust their diet, daily routines, and home environment, and the potential benefits of holistic therapies available around the world. My goal was to empower people with knowledge, helping them make informed choices about treatments that could not only complement conventional medicine but also alleviate some of the extreme side effects of chemotherapy and radiation.

My father spent his first Christmas with me as a widower that same year. Ever the optimist, he had the remarkable ability to make the best of any situation—a trait that had sometimes driven my mother to frustration, especially after Simon's passing.

It was only later that I discovered he had been awarded the Burma Star for his service during the 2nd World War. He never spoke of the horrors he had witnessed or the experiences he had endured, but it was clear he had learned to suppress his emotions. In hindsight, this explained a great deal about his approach to life—Carpe diem was his 'modus operandi'.

He instantly fell in love with Mallorca and its wonderful way of life. Soon after, he asked if I'd mind him buying a place here too. Delighted, we found him a lovely two-bedroom apartment just across from mine, overlooking the golf course in Bendinat. Mallorca suited him perfectly—it reminded him of his expat days, where people of all ages socialised together, enjoying over 300 days of sunshine and warm temperatures for most of the year. He split his time between England and Mallorca, with my new friends welcoming him with open arms, happy for him to join our parties and gatherings. At 80, he was remarkably fit and active, with a naughty sense of humour and a mischievous twinkle in his eye. He loved to dance and would often sweep me or one of my girlfriends onto the dance floor at the many fiestas and celebrations, which he absolutely thrived on. The island was the perfect place for him, and together, we shared countless adventures.

Fast forward 18 years, through the highs and lows of relationships and the roller coaster of life, it was now my father's time to go, at the grand old age of 94. After a gradual three-year decline with dementia, the last six months had been especially challenging. When his condition became too difficult for his carer to manage at home, I had no choice but to place him in a care home.

His final day felt almost orchestrated, as if he had planned it himself. When it became apparent that he didn't have much time left, four of our closest friends—Sarah, Fergus, Eric, and Helen—came to visit. We all surrounded him with love and laughter, reminiscing by his bedside, with the noise and chatter as if he were attending a party. He had stopped speaking the week before, his eyes mostly closed, but as each of us took their turn to speak to him, there was a quiet sense of peace in the air.

Sarah was the last to speak. She gently took his hand and said softly, "Hello, Arthur, it's Sarah. We're here for you." At that moment, his eyes suddenly opened wide for the first time that day. *"We've had such a lovely time together. Thank you for being part of our lives,"* she continued, smiling into his eyes. "The girls asked me to give Bampa a big kiss," she said, referring to her daughters, Atlanta and Summer. He looked up at her, initially startled, before his expression softened into one of pure love and childlike delight, as if he were gazing into the eyes of an angel. It was to be the last twinkle we would see in his eyes. Moments later, he closed them, took a few final, ragged breaths—and he was gone.

Just before his passing, Eric had been telling a funny story. Now, with tears rolling down his cheeks, he asked quite sincerely, *"Do you think my joke was too much for him? I'm so sorry."* We all laughed and cried with mixed emotions. *"Oh, Eric, don't be silly,"* I said, choking back tearful laughter. We all held hands and embraced. I whispered, *"Bon voyage, dear Daddy—we love you."* A nurse poked her head around the door, looking unsure whether we were laughing or crying. *"Mi padre está muerto,"* I said, steadying my voice. My father is gone. I can't even remember what the joke was, but Dad had always loved a good party. It was, in its way, a very fitting end.

Once again, this was a different type of loss - passing at the grand age of 98 through what can typically be called 'natural causes', despite his few years of dementia. A death, but equally a celebration of a life well lived.

I had been praying for him to go swiftly as his condition worsened over his last two weeks. Yet now he was gone; there was the sudden realisation that I had just become an orphan. That may sound odd coming from a middle-aged woman, but regardless, it all felt strangely unsettling. Could

I put my finger on exactly why? Not quite. Fortunately, I was not alone - I had my loving and supportive partner, Hamish, and my sweet little dog Snowy to help me recalibrate. It still took a little time to overcome the stark feeling of separation, especially with no close blood relatives nearby. But he had lived a good, long life. As difficult as it is to lose a parent, there is a certain peace in knowing they had a *"good long innings,"* as my father would have said.

Looking back, I've experienced grief in many forms—each loss unique in its own way, feelings, and emotions. But nothing quite prepares you for the depth of pain that can come with losing a pet. Like so much in life, you don't truly understand it until a little furry bundle of fluff becomes a part of your family.

Few forms of love are as unconditional and uncomplicated as that of a dog—man's best friend. Mine was a very affectionate but particularly needy Bichon Maltese named Snowflake, whom I adopted at four and a half years old and renamed Snowy, to make it more obvious he was a boy. He arrived with constant separation anxiety, which he never overcame, and could rarely be left alone without having a panic attack. He became my sidekick; you got 'us' rather than me - and for many years, part of my own identity. He was quite naughty, and yet such a *"sweet little doggy"* as some would say, coming to pet him with an outstretched hand.... Just before he snapped! More from men coming too close - rarely a woman and never a child (since he'd been brought up with children). That got us into a few embarrassingly difficult scrapes with the police, but it was only ever a very occasional nip. Nevertheless, I loved him dearly.

It was now December 2023. Hamish and I had separated but thankfully had remained firm friends. Snowy was fourteen and had been very fit apart from occasional back pain. He'd started coughing and spluttering a little the week before, which I had thought odd, but was not alarmed. Perhaps he had a cold. Having decided to leave Snowy at home, since we planned quite a challenging hike, we went off for a Sunday walk with a group of friends. Not anticipating that some of our group would get lost, we returned six hours later feeling rather guilty, not having left him for very long before.

He was his usual over-anxious self, letting out a high-pitched, panicked bark. *"Calm down, Snowy, it's okay—we're home,"* I said softly, stroking his head to soothe him. But his barking was suddenly replaced by a fit of coughing and sneezing. My heart dropped as I looked on in horror, as a fine spray of blood spread around us.

"Oh my God," I gasped, turning to Hamish. We exchanged alarmed looks before rushing Snowy straight to the animal hospital. The vet ran tests, but after what felt like a long, anxious wait, he explained there was little they could do until the results came back in a few days. We returned home with a deep sense of unease—he didn't look good at all.

Five days later, the diagnosis confirmed my worst fears: an aggressive cancer spreading through his throat and nose. He didn't have long. My poor little boy.

Never having had children, Snowy had been my surrogate—my fur baby and constant companion for ten years. Despite enduring the losses of my brother and both parents, nothing had quite prepared me for the extremes of emotion I was about to experience. After consulting my trusted vet, I made the heartbreaking decision to forgo chemotherapy.

He advised it would only prolong his suffering, and I couldn't bear to put him through that.

Seven days after the diagnosis, he had an extremely uncomfortable night, semi-asphyxiated and choking for much of it. I took him outside in the early hours, gasping for breath. He looked up at the stars, as if contemplating his life and his not-so-far-away demise. I looked on with a tear running down my face and a lump in my throat. I really wasn't ready for this; I just couldn't bear the thought of losing him.

I spoke with my vet, Nick, the next morning to ask for his advice. It didn't feel right to put him through another difficult night like that. It had been awful to witness. Nick advised it was time.

With a heavy heart and a weight I could scarcely bear, I made the difficult decision that today was the day. I just couldn't let him suffer any longer. At 6 that evening, Nick would come to my home, a nicer and familiar environment for his last moments (than the vet).

I asked Hamish and my friend Sarah to join me for this sad little 'family' outing, and together we set out for one last adventure—to the mountains, to the Lluc Monastery, for a last day out. His best friend Isis trotted beside him, their footsteps falling in rhythm as if it were a normal day out.

Time slowed down around us, stretching each second into something fragile and surreal. A cruel trick of fate—it felt so wrong to choose the hour, and the moment; to end a life that had given me so much joy. *"But he seems fine - are you sure?"* Hamish questioned in sad disbelief, as Snowy snuffled the ground, tail swaying back and forth quite happily, lost in the simple pleasures of the moment and this beautifully sunny day. For an instant, I clung to denial. Nick had reassured me—this was the kindest thing to do after last night; this was love. But as the sun began to descend, I wished with all my heart that I could rewrite time.

We were late getting back to my little cottage in Santa Maria - the awful absurdity that he was due to put to sleep at 6 pm weighing heavily on us as we rushed through traffic. I wound down the window and held him, wiping away my tears - letting him feel the wind on his face for the very last time. I tried my best to retain my composure, so I didn't stress my little boy unnecessarily. I gulped the air with a heavy, beating heart.

Nick, the vet, and Melanie—Snowy's second mummy—were waiting in my casita. We had already kept Nick waiting for thirty minutes. Time was now my enemy, slipping away far too fast, too cruelly.

"Can we wait a little longer?" I asked in desperation. I needed more time, more moments to hold on to, even as they slipped like sand through my fingers. Nick stepped outside with quict understanding, leaving us for a few final moments.

I offered Snowy a few last treats—sausages, his favourite, and even a few morsels of chocolate, a forbidden indulgence he was never allowed. He sniffed at it, his curiosity flickering through the haze of weariness. I could almost hear his bemused thought—*Now you give me chocolate?*

He chewed slowly, sensing the weight of the air and the sorrow that clung to me. Each second stretched unbearably, my heart pounding against the walls of my chest, while a cold dread settled over me like a shroud.

I was fortunate to have Hamish and Melanie with me to hold my hand. They were naturally also very emotional. I couldn't delay any longer and lay him down gently on the sheepskin rug, his favourite spot in front of the fireplace - whispering to him as soothingly as I could muster.

He was calm, serene, even—as if he understood. As if he had already made his peace.

I cradled his face in my hands, gazing into his deep, knowing, hazel eyes; my vision blurred with tears. Goodbye, my darling Snowflake, I choked, my voice breaking as Nick gently and caringly administered the two injections, easing him into his final sleep.

I whispered into his ear, my fingers tracing the soft white fur I had stroked a thousand times before. I thanked him for his unwavering love, for the laughter he inspired, and for the countless adventures we shared.

We wept together, our hands resting on his still, lifeless little body. He looked as though he was merely sleeping, lost in some peaceful dream. A kinder passing than the human experience, I reflected. Still gut-wrenching and unbearably sad—but merciful, at least, when the suffering has become too much to bear.

Snowy's death hit me like a cannonball, rather untimely, just one week before Christmas 2023. I navigated the festivities with a brave face, keeping myself busy with my twin brother Oliver and my niece Sofiia, visiting from the UK.

But after they left, I spiralled downhill rapidly. Once again, I was very fortunate to have Hamish as my rock. I became quite depressed, bursting into tears randomly. Even when out cycling with Hamish and his cycling group, I'd find myself welling up and crying behind my glasses – I just couldn't pull myself together.

Having had numerous experiences of death up to now, this felt a very extreme reaction. But I couldn't shift it; I was not myself. A mixture of other circumstances, added to the wrong hormone treatment (I subsequently ascertained), had made the dive much deeper.

Grief is a weight best carried with the help of others. In the aftermath of Snowy's passing, I found solace in Hamish, who had loved him as much as I and understood the depths of my sorrow. Support arrived in unexpected ways. My friend Jacquie, sensing my struggle, urged me to stop the HRT treatment, sharing how it had once pulled her into a quiet despair and even paranoia. More than that, she offered me a lifeline—inviting me to be her test case as she trained in QEC Therapy (Quantum Energy Counselling). The timing felt almost divinely guided, as though the universe had placed this opportunity in my path just when I needed it most.

And so, through quiet sessions and gentle shifts, I began to move through the grief—not past it, for I still miss him achingly—but through it. The sharp edges softened; the seemingly unbearable weight lightened. Healing is not about forgetting; it is about learning to carry the love we had for our loved one without being crushed by the loss.

Having mentioned Snowy, it wouldn't feel right not to acknowledge the passing of his little fur-brother, Neo, just four months later. He had meowed his way into my life two years earlier as a frail, very unwell, tiny black kitten. We soon discovered that he had been born with a heart defect, clearly the reason he had been abandoned as the runt of his litter.

Despite his small size and fragile heart, a lot of love and attention transformed him into a feisty and energetic little boy. Snowy, having spent most of his life chasing cats, made for a tricky start, but over time, the two became inseparable. They wrestled and tussled constantly; their playful antics were hilarious to witness. After Snowy's death, Neo seemed to miss his companion deeply. For weeks, he would peer out the door, searching for his fur-brother, as if hoping he might return.

Although I had been warned he wouldn't make old bones due to his heart condition, Neo's passing was still deeply heartbreaking. That Saturday morning, he had curled up with me for much longer than usual—something I had noted as unusual at the time. When I found him in the garden that afternoon, lying immobile and yowling in distress, the shock was no less devastating. It would have been easier, in some ways, to let the vet handle it without me, but I couldn't do that. I wanted to be there for him in his final moments—to comfort him, to let him see his mummy's face as his last, instead of a stranger in a white coat. As he slipped away under the injection, I looked into his pained, trusting eyes and whispered, *"Goodbye, little one. Thank you for being in my life. We loved you so much. Go and be with your brother."*

It's remarkable how these small fur babies weave their way so deeply into our hearts. Neo's loss left another scar upon my heart—one that will remain with me forever, holding its special place alongside my other loved ones who have passed.

Naturally, I think of them all quite often, with memories surfacing at different moments. Over time, I've come to believe that when a sudden, strong feeling or thought of a loved one arises, it is their soul checking in, making their presence known. On one particular day, a few years after I arrived in Mallorca, I was rushing to leave the house to meet my friend Monique, a psychic. As I was walking down the corridor, I suddenly caught a strong scent of roses and immediately thought of my mother. But in my hurry, I dismissed it as my imagination and rushed out of the house. (There were no roses or any other possible source at that time.) Later, over lunch, Monique paused our conversation to say, 'Before I forget, I need to tell you something. Earlier today, you had a moment when you smelled a fragrance of flowers and thought of your mother, but you brushed it aside, assuming it was just your imagination. Well, it wasn't-it was her, reminding you that she is watching over you and she loves you very much.' Roses were her favourite flower - that confirmation made me much more aware of these subtle signs from then on.

My story up to now has been focused on my physical losses, which all took their toll on my heart and soul. What I haven't touched upon is the impact of a relationship breakup, of which I have inevitably had quite a few. Whether it be a partner, family member, or a friend, it can feel like grief when you lose someone from your life, even if it's not of a permanent life-and-death nature. It is still loss and separation. Even financial losses, loss of status, or even a job can bring on similar feelings.

Up to now, I have shared my journey of grief and loss, in the hope it will bring some reassurance and comfort that it is possible to get through it, no matter how hard it is at the time. But I will now focus on sharing what I have learned about how to survive and cope amid one of the darkest moments of anyone's life. I have compiled some practical tips which I have gleaned from my own experiences, as well as from many other sources and wise counsel along the way.

Whatever the cause, grief is such a tumultuous roller coaster ride, and we can all react differently. After the initial trauma and shock, one can become rather numb, and everything can appear rather surreal, just going through the very slow motions of day-to-day life. Deep rage can follow, or the feeling of abandonment, which can be amplified considerably if living alone, or possibly even with no close relations or friends nearby.

Some people don't wish to deal with their sorrow and instead bury their heads in the sand, keeping themselves busy, trying to shut out the feelings and the pain. Of course, these are all coping mechanisms, and although it may seem easier to occupy ourselves in constant activities to take our minds off our sadness, this can make the route to healing much more difficult.

When you feel weak, vulnerable, and in grief, you will inevitably feel helpless. Pacing thoughts, sleepless nights, desperate moments. But allowing yourself to feel vulnerable is a natural part of the grieving-and-healing process, providing a headspace to sort through the rollercoaster range of emotions that are present when we experience loss.

Unless we listen to where we are in the moment, the emotions we experience will only grow in intensity, and feelings will manifest in more powerful and less comfortable ways. Once we consciously acknowledge that these emotions are present, however, we can soothe the sorrow of the moment. You need to ride out the emotional wave. In so doing, we become more open to our natural ability to heal ourselves. It's like going through the death, burial, and rebirth process of our soul each time.

It's important not to withdraw completely, facing this difficult time alone in silence and solitude. While it may be tempting to immerse yourself in self-pity and isolation, closing yourself off can lead to deep despair and even severe depression. Moreover, don't listen to the negative chatter in your head telling you that you'll be a burden or that others will feel sorry for you. Be assured, those close to you wish to help, but can feel helpless not knowing how to.

Reach out to a close family member or friend, whether for practical help, advice, motivation, or simply companionship. Let them know what you need, even if it's just someone to sit with you in silence. Spending time with others can provide the strength and healing necessary to regain some sense of normality. You don't have to carry this burden alone - so reach out and let people in. It can also help forge closer bonds. This is not just about getting through it; it's a journey back to you.

If you don't feel that you have someone you're able to confide in, consider reaching out to a grief counsellor, a community helpline, or a holistic practitioner. If you don't know one personally, someone in your circle—perhaps a yoga enthusiast—may be able to recommend one. You could also try to find a local Death Cafe – a global movement that invites people to drink tea, eat cake, and talk about death, sharing with others who are going through the same process.

If you're spiritually inclined, don't forget to ask your angels or guides for support. If not, simply ask the universe for help and guidance—you might be surprised what comes back to you, in the most unimaginable ways.

Healing cannot be rushed. Dip your toe in, and if it feels right, do it. If it doesn't, don't. Don't try to do too much - this period of grieving is not the best time to make any major decisions if they can be avoided. So just put them on the side until you are ready.

It's also clearly important to eat. If you don't feel up to it, just try eating a little, as often as possible. Fresh, healthy food is super important to help the body regain strength and vitality, rather than opting for ultra-processed convenience foods. Homemade smoothies with nutritious seeds and powders are quick, easy, and nutritious, as are homemade soups, which can be made in batches and frozen. If you can't cook, buy some ready-made meals from the fresh section, rather than frozen. Adding a few of your favourite treats can also help put a little smile on your face.

Equally, daily exercise, of some sort, is essential. Go for regular walks in nature and practice some mindfulness techniques of just appreciating the beauty of nature.

Be gentle with yourself - this is a time of change and transformation. Dig down into your heart and feel your way forward. Honour your grief and recognise that one day you might feel strong, the next you could be back on the floor, feeling it as viscerally as a full-frontal assault. Grieving comes in waves that will roll in and out, as something equally natural as the ebb and flow of the tide—sometimes gentle, sometimes overwhelming, but always a part of the rhythm of life.

Suffering and grief give rise to seeking. When you are finally able to come to terms with it, you will experience the most profound growth—it expands your awareness and reconnects you to the universal source of wisdom within. You must sit with it, honour it, and allow these feelings to move through you.

Releasing negative emotions often becomes easier when you give them a physical or tangible form: try keeping a journal or writing a letter to yourself or to the one you've lost. Moreover, starting a gratitude journal is a wonderful tool for finding positivity in daily life, listing three things each day you're grateful for. Can't think of anything right now? That's ok - try recalling a happy memory, your favourite song or film, or write down the name of someone who makes you laugh. Think of something different each day.

Tapping (EFT) can also be a powerful tool; you can learn it online or, even better, seek out a local EFT therapist. This practice can help shift your pain, making it more manageable.

When we find ourselves in the depths of darkness, feeling as if our world is falling apart, we fail to see that pain and suffering are catalysts for growth. Just as a caterpillar must first retreat into its chrysalis before transforming into a butterfly, struggle is an essential part of every soul's evolution. Within the darkness of the cocoon, the caterpillar has no awareness of the transformation that lies just up ahead. Yet, on the other side of that darkness and struggle, something extraordinary awaits—the emergence of a breathtakingly beautiful being, ready to spread its wings and soar.

Grief is ultimately humanity's greatest teacher - our soul becomes more expansive, wiser, and stronger for it. Like a muscle that is torn with the strain of exercise, with all the aches and pains, it will grow back so much bigger and stronger.

So don't put yourself under pressure. Although you won't feel it at the time, you're stronger than you realise; hang on in there. There will eventually be a moment when you can raise your head above the clouds and start looking towards the rainbow, and your future. Slowly, but surely, just take baby steps forward. When you're ready, you can then decide what you want to do next. Ask yourself, *"Where do I want to be? What do I want to do?"* What do you want to create?

Once that transition occurs and you choose to move forward, the results will be swift. In doing so, there is no dilution in the importance of what you've lost, no diminishing its value. But don't fear leaving it behind, as what is important is moving forward and commencing the next chapter of your life.

I read these two passages recently and felt these words provide a comforting analogy to the grieving process.

Grief is like glitter

You can throw a handful of glitter into the air, but when you come to clean it up, you will never get it all - it will always be there somewhere, hiding in corners.

In time, these shards of grief will make you glad when you come across them, as they will remind you of the love and the amazing times you shared with your loved one.

Not apart from you, but a part of you....... as you now go forward.

– adapted from the original quote *by Kevin Pádraig.*

'Glass Balloon' from the book When I Am Gone, by *Becky Hemsley*

So fragile and yet so heavy.

I'm terrified to let it go. In case it breaks, smashes. And I have nothing left.

I can't deflate it.

But it's weighing me down and the longer I hold it, the sooner I feel like I'll buckle under the weight of it.

And how do I explain to others that I am carrying something so delicate yet so substantial? How do I ask them to help me carry this thing that they cannot see?

Perhaps I'm not supposed to let it go.

Perhaps I'm supposed to tie it to my heart and carry it around forever. And it will remain as heavy and as fragile as it has always been, but I will get used to carrying it.

I will learn how to hold it on the difficult days, rather than letting it hold me.

I will learn how to let it lift me up rather than letting it weigh me down.

I will learn how to explain it to others rather than shouldering the weight in silence.

And as time goes on, maybe...Just maybe...

I will figure out how to let it fly.

No matter what you grieve, or how you grieve, your glass balloon is valid.

Painful as it all was at the time, there is no doubt I have grown the most out of my most tragic experiences. Each one was heart-wrenching and so very hard to navigate. None is easier to deal with than others - they are all very different. But with the healing of time and coming to terms with the feelings and the loss of that separation, I now recognise that these experiences have made me the person I am today. Helping to dissolve my ego, raise my wisdom, build intimacy with my fears, and open my heart to greater love and compassion. We become better people, which ultimately leads us to become our most authentic selves and the best version of ourselves.

It's when we learn how to transmute the suffering so that the pain turns to purpose that it can become a journey to enlightenment of some sort or other. A source of wisdom and guidance to help others in their time of need, and even potentially a source of inspiration to give back to our community in some way, no matter how small. We are all unique and important pieces in the puzzle of this game we call life.

Every loss has made a mark on my soul. I carry them all with me.

These wounds will soften with time. But they become a part of your soul. And you can perhaps then reframe that loss and see it instead as a gain. A reminder of the love you had for another soul. My father used to have a favourite adage from Alfred Lord Tennyson: *It is better to have loved and lost than to have never loved at all.*

This is true on so many levels. With deep love comes deep loss and deep grief - but would I exchange any of that grief for not having had the love of - and from - Simon or my parents? Or Snowy or Neo? The loss of them hurt beyond words - but would I change it? No, not for anything.

In this way, we can - or at least can try, in the darkest of moments - to look at grief as almost a privilege to have experienced, for it is the extreme essence of love. It then comes down to what we take away from it, which is inextricably linked to the richness of life itself.

Two decades after losing my beloved mother, Patricia, I channelled my grief into purpose, launching Wellness Traveller—an online travel platform dedicated to holistic health and wellness. More than just a booking site, it is a carefully curated collection of hotels, retreats, and transformative experiences, and most importantly to me, an array of truly gifted holistic practitioners who can help people to heal.

Though we are currently focused on the Balearics, my partners and I dream of something greater—a global movement where wellness is not just a privilege but an accessible, deeply personal journey for all.

In time, we aim to set up the Patricia Butler Charitable Foundation to assist underprivileged individuals with chronic health conditions to gain access to integrative therapies, to help support their treatments, and to rebalance their bodies holistically.

We have all loved, and we have all lost. Sometimes we strive, and sometimes we thrive. I am ultimately the sum of all my experiences. I am bigger and stronger for all of them. I appreciate each moment so much more for all these times of strife and sadness, with some rather bittersweet memories; living with my dear father Arthur's motto in the back of my mind - Carpe diem, seize the day! For we never know when our light will be extinguished - so I endeavour to shine it as brightly as I can, each and every day.

Death, after all, is inevitable, and I like to believe, is a transition that takes us on to our next and greatest adventure of all.

In memory of my loved ones passed – Simon, Mum, Dad, Snowy and Neo - thank you for being part of the rich tapestry of my life.

Nothing you love is lost

Bruce Coville

"Nothing you love is lost.

Not really.

Things, people—they always go away, sooner or later.

You can't hold them, any more than you can hold moonlight.

But if they've touched you, if they're inside you, then they're still yours.

The only things you ever really have are the ones you hold inside your heart."

~Jeremy Thatcher, Dragon Hatcher: A Magic Shop Book (c) 1991~

Signs of Life

BY VICKI MCLEOD

Oesophagus cancer is a pretty shitty way to die, especially if one of the things you loved most in life was eating and drinking. You cannot swallow anymore and rely on a feeding bag; everyone blames you for "bringing cancer upon yourself" because you ate too much processed meat in the 90s or drank too much whisky at parties. But then there will be some other guy who only ate that for breakfast, lunch, and dinner who lives until he's 103, so go figure that one out.

I was with my Dad when he died, suffering from this pernicious cancer. The last thing he ate was a mouthful of yoghurt and two blueberries, and he took a really long time to eat them. It had become obvious over the days leading up to his death that he *"wasn't very well,"* but still my family couldn't quite bring themselves to say it out loud, that he was definitely dying. Or maybe we just didn't recognise the signs. How many other dying people had we ever been in contact with? For me, none.

It came as quite a surprise then that my Dad upped and died that Sunday evening in his home in the mountains of Mallorca, with me and his wife and her daughter by his side. He was really angry about getting sick, and when he died, he did not go quietly. It was a noisy death. In his final moments, he grasped for lungfuls of air as if he were underwater, but each exhalation was longer than the one before until there was finally just one long out-breath that just kept going… What followed was a solemn, calm energy hanging in the air. It wasn't like the feeling you have when there is a thunderstorm on the way or that prickly static electricity you get when you rub a balloon on your hair and watch it rise upwards, but there was a deep, rich silence that filled the room.

We use countless euphemisms to describe death: passed away, succumbed, slipped away, entered eternal rest, gone to a better place, or crossed over. Some may make you laugh, others cringe, but one will feel right for you. For me, it's best to say the "D" word and be done with it.

We can't escape death, so why don't we talk about it more? We are disconnected from so many natural processes now in our lives; we don't kill the chicken that we roast in the oven, many of us choose to not give birth to our babies naturally, and we give away the job of preparing the bodies of our dead loved ones to undertakers. In short, we don't seem to want to get our hands dirty. I think that is because we are afraid of experiencing the very profound feelings of pain, guilt, and despair. We choose to be in a numbed condition.

And we do that by slipping a veil over our truth. But what we are trying to avoid cannot be avoided, and every single one of us will experience loss and grief in our lifetime.

We are frightened to remind a grieving person of their pain by bringing up their loss, so we skirt around the subject for fear of upsetting them. But they are already upset, aren't they? A very long time ago, I interviewed a mother whose child had died when she was only 3 years old. I asked her, *"What can people do to help you?"* and she replied, *"Never stop talking about my daughter, because when you do, that is when she has truly died."* What if you tried instead to connect through a few words, something as simple as *"I'm so sorry for your loss."* That could be enough to make contact. You don't need to overthink your words; just speak from your heart, but don't make it about you, and don't make assumptions about how they are feeling. Express sympathy. Or if you feel you have the strength to go deeper, you can be empathic. *"I can't imagine how hard this must be for you, but I'm here to listen."*

This is true; until you consciously go through a loss, you can't imagine how it feels. Imagining the feelings of grief is like expecting a first baby. You can read all the baby and parenting books that you like, but until you have that child in your arms, you cannot conceive of the emotions that you will have. There are no words that adequately describe it; you simply have to be present and feel. And just like having a baby, grief changes you permanently. It is up to you if that is a downgrade or an improvement on the current model.

There's a lot of talk about the grieving process as if it is linear and there are clear stages that you go through, but in my own experience of loss and grieving, there is no clear path. It is a personal journey that you are on, but you don't need to travel solo. There are many passengers on a plane, but we aren't all turning left when we board, but the journey is the same, but the experience for each of us is different. This can make the prospect terrifying; you might ask yourself, *"How can I cope with this? What will it feel like? I don't know what to do or who to talk to,"* and so many other questions, but you will have to do it anyway, so accepting the fact that you are going to grieve in your life is crucial.

But I didn't know that when my Dad died.

When my father died, it was actually a shock. Yes, we knew he was terminally ill, but he had been given some months to live, and I had expected to have time with him. As it was, I left a job on the Friday with the intention of doing that, and he was dead 48 hours later.

The Evolution of Grief

I've learned now that the first days after a loss, you cannot have expectations of yourself. How you will behave and what you will do may come as a surprise. For some of us, we will go into a full "coping mode" where all the arrangements and details that come up will keep us blissfully busy, occupying the mind fully. There will be lists upon lists of things to do. But, just like when you have that baby, when you experience a loss, like the death of someone who you cared for, you cannot be sure that you will get out of the house, showered and ready to face the world. You may find yourself in your dressing gown, drinking the tenth cup of tea of the day and mindlessly watching daytime TV with no memory of anything and no concept of the time that has passed. Both approaches serve a purpose. You are either delaying the effect of the loss on your heart and soul, or you are deflecting it.

There comes a time when you will step into that grief. When I did that, I howled. I howled in the car, I howled in the bathroom, and I howled in my bedroom, but it took some practice to do it in public, which, to continue the *"having a baby"* analogy, is a bit like breastfeeding; people stare when you do it in public. I noticed that if I spoke about my Dad, my eyes would automatically fill with tears, and whoever I was speaking to would have one of three reactions: awkwardness, sympathy, or flat-out avoidance. I learned that it didn't matter what those responses were because I needed to let the tears out. In some societies, showing emotion is not acceptable; bottling up and not showing your feelings is the correct thing to do, and I suppose that is because being vulnerable is risky; it opens you up to ridicule and to exploitation. But think about it, do you really want people in your life who would laugh at your tears or take advantage of your deepest feelings? No, the answer is no. And showing your feelings is a tribute to the person that you have lost, so show them, express them, talk about them, however weird and strange and hard that feels at the beginning, it gets easier to talk, and it's better out than in. There was, however, a balance that I needed to strike, a line that I discovered I couldn't cross. I found that I could not watch any movie where, after you are made to care for them, the main characters then die. Deliberately experiencing sadness was not, and still isn't, a source of entertainment for me. But perversely, I can listen to the saddest music, and that was, and still is, a comfort and a wonderful way to connect to my father and memories of him.

Finding Meaning

For others, they find comfort in signs. A feather, a rainbow, a cloud, a breeze, a dream, a flickering light, a scent, and so many more, but the one that became connected to the death of my Dad, was butterflies. Gigantic red butterflies who visited his wife repeatedly in the days after he died. When she told me, I didn't believe her, and at the same time I was jealous.

Why weren't they coming to see me? Why wasn't I getting the visits? In his defence, he came to visit me in a dream that first week. He was full of life and so healthy and happy in my slumber, and it gave me great happiness to see him, but I knew on a practical level that this was just my brain working through memories... But the butterflies? Surely his wife was imagining that.

A few weeks after he had been cremated, we took my Dad's ashes for breakfast. We went to a cafe in Port Andratx, which he loved to go to, and had a *"Fat Boy's Breakfast"* featuring all the things that may or may not have contributed to his cancer: bacon, sausages, fried food... The plan had been to eat breakfast in his honour and then take his ashes out and scatter them at sea from his boat. There were several of us at the table, many of the people that my Dad would have called his closest friends and loved ones, his wife and some of her children, and some of my family. The weather that day was terrible, heavy rain, which did not bode well for a sail, but still we were going to do it. As we sat in the cafe, as soon as the food was served, a very large red butterfly flew in and circled the table for what seemed to be several minutes. We sat there, unable to say a thing to each other, and watched it flutter around and around the table. Where had it come from? It was pouring with rain outside. Why did this huge butterfly only circle our table?

How do you explain this? I don't know if you can. But the butterflies, despite me not believing in them, continued to show up for my Dad's wife and for me, and still do. What does it mean? I don't know, but I do know that when they appear, I think of him, and that makes me smile, and that, in itself, is a good thing.

Learning to Live in the New Reality

Reflecting on the time when my father died, I see now that I was not a stranger to grief. I had already experienced the process of loss and readjustment when, in the space of a year, my parents had divorced, and I had separated from a long-term partner, moved house, and changed jobs. When these events happened, in my twenties, I was devastated and had to rebuild my life from one day to the next. It was then that I learned that there is no one way to feel after a huge loss or change. I gave myself permission to have all the feelings. I didn't judge myself for how I felt. And I didn't try to rush myself, although I was surprised at how long it was before I started to feel happier and even longer to notice that I wasn't waking up every morning feeling sad. I learned then to not have expectations of how long the process would take, as judging myself was not in any way helpful to the recovery, which I so badly needed.

What did help me was to write my feelings down. I carried a notebook with me wherever I went, and I would read back my thoughts to try to make a road map of events to really understand what had happened. You don't have to be brave; you have to be able to be aware of yourself and your feelings and let them flow, and writing has helped me with that. I found as well that when I started the practice of *"self-care"* (which in the 90s didn't really exist), I discovered a little pocket in each day where I would feel a bit less terrible. I started to plan something daily that was just for me, something that I would look forward to: meeting a friend for a coffee, getting a massage, or making a meal that I loved. Gently prioritising my wishes really helped. I also found the importance of movement and exercise. Whatever it was, I made it happen daily. And this I now understand has a direct impact on my brain chemistry and my hormones, which can stimulate feelings of well-being and joy.

It wasn't until recently that I realised that you could grieve not only for loved ones who have died, but also for a life that has completely changed. Sometimes that change is within your control, and sometimes it is not, but your response to the change is in your hands. I see this as an opportunity to look at the things that matter to me the most; it's a wonderful reminder that you are capable of giving and receiving unlimited love and giving yourself grace and the space to assimilate the new changes.

This year I have had a new grief to navigate, that of my daughter leaving home to study abroad at university. Although I knew I would miss her, I did not appreciate that I would again go through a grieving process, and it floored me. My work productivity collapsed as I was not able to concentrate on my projects or find any creative spark to draw on. I felt exhausted, depressed, and without any motivation. It took me a few weeks before I realised I was going through the same feelings as when my father died. *"Aha!"* I thought, *"This is grief again. Hello, old friend."*

Although I can't tell you, *"Hey, grief is fantastic; you should get some,"* I do feel that the life events that I have had, which pushed me through this process, have made me grow as an individual, as a friend, as a wife, and as a parent. The rawness and vulnerability of loss can leave you feeling bitter and angry; you can ask yourself, *"Why ME?"* but the real question you should be asking is, *"Why NOT me?"* Asking those questions of yourself will bring answers, and then when someone you love needs support through their grief, you can be there for them. My capacity to support others has increased, and that in itself gives meaning to life events. I do not shy away from discussions about death and dying, and I hope that I can be a safe place for someone needing to talk.

When Longfellow wrote, [1]

"There is no grief like the grief that does not speak,"

he understood the weight of silence.

Speaking about loss—sharing your feelings, your memories, and even your tears—can transform grief into a source of connection and strength. The emotions we carry, though heavy, are personal signs of life, proof that we are still here, still loving, still learning.

Like butterflies, feathers, or rainbows, those feelings remind us to embrace the extraordinary adventure we are all on. When you are ready, stand tall and go "all in" for life.

Life's lessons, such as loss and the grief of that loss, have much to teach us if we are willing to listen.

> "What we once enjoyed and deeply loved we can never lose, for all that we love deeply becomes a part of us."
>
> Helen Keller

Grief, in its rawness, reminds us of our capacity to love profoundly and to endure.

Grief will walk beside you, but it does not have to hold you back

1. American - Poet February 27, 1807 - March 24, 1882

Life Goes On

LINDA LEDWIDGE

Life is a journey of constant change—adjustments, gains, and losses.

With each shift, we adapt, transform, and **BE***come*.

And each time, we **BE***come more*.

Think of the caterpillar transforming into a butterfly. How does this small, unassuming creature evolve into something so strikingly beautiful? It grows, it changes, it **BE***comes*. Its very being embodies transformation.

In our society, we call this transformation "the grief process."

Grief is just a word—five simple letters—but oh, the power we give it.

Society teaches us that grief follows the loss of a loved one, that it is a feeling we all share. And yet, grief is not merely a feeling—it is a process;

one we experience repeatedly throughout our lives in varying degrees, often without realising it. More often than not, we don't name it as grief until someone we love gains their Angel Wings and we are told, *"It's ok, you are grieving."*

The grieving process that follows the death of someone we love is often the catalyst that sends us spiralling-however, if we are lucky, it can also lead us to a profound realisation that grief, when we allow it, can be transformative.

There have been many times in my life when I have gone through what I call "a storm," only to come out the other side feeling as though it happened to someone else. Each time, I compartmentalised the experience, tucked it away in a box never to be opened, and moved on to the next chapter. I believe we all do this to some degree throughout our lives.

I grew up in Scotland with traditional family values, where my extended family was my immediate family. Aunts, uncles, and cousins were a constant presence in my life. We spent weekends and holidays together, sharing the most amazing times—along with some incredible disagreements and fallouts, especially at New Year when everyone had a bit too much to drink!

Growing up, my extended family was my strong foundation, my Mum, Dad, Terry, Sandra, & Susan, my brother and sisters, were my pillars, my strength when I needed it.

After my Gran passed, or as I like to think of it, gained her Angel Wings, my aunts and uncles took on the task of keeping our traditions alive, inevitably, we didn't gather as often. We always made the effort to come together for Christmas, New Year, weddings, christenings, and, of course, funerals. We continue to do so to this day. Even though we're now scattered across the globe, we find ways to reunite whenever we can. Video calls have made it easier to stay connected.

My kids, my Munchkins, remain close to their aunts, uncles, and cousins, despite living in another country. They have strong foundations too. It may not be in quite the same way I experienced growing up, all the same, they remain a part of each other's lives. My identity was—and still is—rooted in my family.

The first memory I have of experiencing grief over losing someone I loved was when my Granda gained his Angel Wings. I was about 11 years old, and I recall the profound sense of loss, feeling that my world had changed in ways I couldn't comprehend. Granda had been ill with stomach cancer, though I didn't understand it at the time. I just knew he was frequently in and out of the hospital, always returning home—until he didn't. I remember walking to the shopping centre from my house, wondering, *"What happens now?" "Are we still going to be a family?" "Where did he go?"* Looking back, I realise that I was grieving, even though I was too young to recognise it.

The first time I truly understood grief was when my cousin Matt gained his Angel Wings at 21, such a young age. He had visited us about a week before because he was in Scotland with his girlfriend. He had moved "down south" as we liked to say. Matt used to tease me because I was too scared to watch horror movies, although I knew he was teasing and didn't mean any of it. I remember him to this day so full of life—he was my idol. Everything I wanted to be. Happy, fun, and bursting with energy. Just pure joy—that's how I remember him, and I like it that way. Not a day goes by when he isn't in my thoughts.

Not long after Matt gained his Angel Wings, my Gran gained hers. I was only 17 and my world turned upside down. Gran and I had been on a holiday that summer to visit Aunt Beattie, who lived in Devon, and it was so much fun. It was the only time Gran and I had been away together, just the two of us. I cherish that memory.

Gran was *our cornerstone*, the one our family depended on. She gave us all direction and purpose, and without her, everything felt unsteady.

For many, many years after her passing, I sent my Mum a bouquet of flowers on the Angelversary of her death. We never spoke about it, still, I knew it brought her comfort- just knowing that I remembered Gran too and was thinking of her.

When I married and had my own Munchkins, *my own wee family*, I added another storey to my family's building. Thankfully, we had strong foundations.

Looking back, I can see how *losing* these people shaped my world. Nevertheless at the time, I didn't. I pushed it all away and carried on- just as I have done with so many things over the years. No one had ever taught me how to navigate these deeply important parts of life's journey.

I weathered many *storms* over the years and came through them all, or did I? Did I ever truly come through them? On some level, yes. On another level, I only made it part of the way through. I never fully completed the *grieving process*- never allowed myself to transform completely.

Now I understand that this is part of life's journey.

And then, on the 18th of February 2014, everything changed.

That year had not started well for my family or me. In January, after 24 years together, my husband, Peter, and I made the painful decision to separate. We both knew that it was the right thing to do, although that didn't make it any easier. Then, in the first week of February, my youngest sister was diagnosed with late-stage lung cancer. The news devastated us all, especially my Dad, who was already chronically ill.

At the time, I was working as a holistic therapist, incorporating my midwifery experience to provide antenatal classes and natural childbirth classes to pregnant women who wanted an English-speaking midwife. I worked from a practice in Palma and conducted online sessions with clients from all over the world. On the morning of February 18th, I had a two-hour session scheduled for 10:00 with a client who lives in America. At 9:50, my brother-in-law called. His words rocked my world: my Dad had gained his Angel Wings that morning.

I was in shock. He had been ill for years, although his passing was unexpected. Thank goodness my friend Trina had stayed over the night before—I had no idea what to do. My client was already online waiting for her session. I switched to autopilot. I told Trina I'd try to cut the session short, although it would depend on the client. So I walked into the room, put on my *therapist* hat, and carried on.

All I remember is that the session went really well. The client got what she needed. And the moment it ended, I fell apart.

What do I do?

I had to tell my Munchkins—my kids. Thankfully, they had seen their Granda Pops just two weeks earlier, even so this news would devastate them. Trina helped me pull myself together. I called Peter, and he, thankfully, took over and arranged for me to fly to Scotland the next morning. That evening, I went to tell the kids. The entire evening is a blur. I was numb—but not numb. Feeling so much that my body and mind couldn't process or handle it. Outwardly, I functioned. Somehow, I made it to the airport the next morning and got on the plane. I remember turning to Peter and saying, *"I don't think I can do this."*

Inside, I was in turmoil. I felt broken. *"Who was I without my Dad?"* He was *my* cornerstone, my anchor.

I was lucky though, I had tools. I had spent my life researching, studying, and training in holistic therapies. I could do this. I would be okay.

"Wouldn't I?"

2014 was one of the most challenging and memorable years of my life-and so much of it is a blur. There are entire periods I can't recall with any kind of clarity at all.

I went to Mum, my brother Terry, and my sisters, Sandra and Susan. The funeral arrangements were made—it was awful. I felt lost. My anchor had always been Dad, and now I had nothing to hold on to.

We were all together, but we struggled to support each other. We were all broken. And with my baby sister so ill, we couldn't even grieve properly for Dad—we had to be there for her.

And Mum—poor Mum. I don't know how she got through it. I understood why she was so angry. From that day on, I can't remember a time when she wasn't angry.

Without our extended/immediate family, we would have struggled even more than we did. They were there for us, supporting us in any way they could. That's just what we did for each other. They were the strong foundations.

I stayed with Mum for about five weeks, doing what I could to support her. Just being there was all I could offer. I felt so empty and lost; I could not imagine what she was going through.

Back in Mallorca, my life was in turmoil. I no longer understood what was happening around me. I did my best to work, to keep myself and my Munchkins as steady as possible. Looking back, I know I didn't do it very well – and I have since forgiven myself. I had to. Without that forgiveness, I wouldn't have been able to heal.

Over the next five months, I travelled back and forth between Scotland and Mallorca as my sister underwent chemotherapy and grew weaker. We were all so angry at life, at God, at the universe, at anything and everything you can be angry at in times like these.

I threw myself into doing whatever I could to help Susan. I wanted to try everything. We all did.

As a nurse, I had spent over a year working in an oncology unit, caring for patients undergoing chemotherapy. Some went into remission, and we all celebrated their recovery; others I cared for through their last months, weeks, and days, feeling privileged to support them and their families through such profound moments in their lives. And, of course, we also grieved alongside them.

The time I spent with my sister was one of the greatest learning experiences of my life. Susan and I spent time talking about our fears, our dreams, our desires, and our regrets. Susan struggled deeply with the things in her life that she felt she had left undone. She had 3 Munchkins who needed her, and she had been told that, very soon, she was not going to be there for them. She had been with Michael since school; they were childhood sweethearts. How could she leave him?

I couldn't accept that she wouldn't come through this. My beliefs would not allow it. I *knew* she could. Now though, I understand that what I believe, and what I know, is not enough. No matter how much we love someone, they have their own road to travel. What I do know is how grateful I am that I was part of her story, her journey, and that she was part of mine.

We faced our greatest fears together. We did our best to squash hers, and she made me promise that I would conquer mine. Fear, she said, had no place in my life.

Since childhood, I had been terrified of water. I would not go into a pool or the sea above waist height. I had an insane fear of horses. And the thought of living alone? Unthinkable!

Over the next 5 years, I kept my promise. I took a diving course and earned my PADI® Open Water Diver certification. Now, I *love* taking my Mini-munchkins swimming in the sea and pool. I went horse riding-twice! -and can now be around horses without fear. I live on my own...and I *love* it!

I watched Susan move through it all, the shock, the anger, the denial, the guilt, the depression, the bargaining, and finally, the acceptance. There were so many more stages, and not necessarily in that order. She moved back and forth between them every single day.

The day before she gained her Angel wings, I was lying beside her on the bed. She was so weak at this point that we took turns lying with her and chatting or just simply being at her side. We were lying quietly when she suddenly turned to me, gave me the biggest kiss, and told me she loved me.

She said, *"I'm ready."*

My heart shattered into a million pieces. I looked at her; I held her close and told her we were all here. And when she felt it was time, we would be right by her side-loving her, supporting her, always.

I feel incredibly blessed to have spent that precious time with Susan. It was the hardest experience I have ever faced and also the most humbling.

And so, on the 3rd of August 2014-just over 23 weeks after we lost Dad-Susan gained her Angel Wings and went to join him.

I was already reeling from everything that had happened that year. And now we had lost my baby sister. Through the heartbreak, Terry, Sandra, and I did everything we could to hold it together-for Mum, for Susan's husband, and for her Munchkins.

I have no words to truly describe it. Even now, the feeling is raw.

Most of the time I think of Susan with so much love and joy that my heart sings, that said, there are times when that heartbreaking, gut-wrenching sense of loss is hard to forget.

When I returned to Mallorca, I was truly lost. If not for my family, my Munchkins, and my friends, I'm not sure I would have made it through.

That's the thing about grief, though—*life goes on.*

You may not want it to. You may ask yourself, as I did, *"How can life go on? How do people not realise that the world has ended as I knew it? How do I go on?"*

Somehow, you do. You find a way. It takes time, and there are moments when you feel you simply can't go on. And then, you do.

The most important thing is *how* you get through it. And that, I was about to learn, is the greatest lesson of all.

In 2014, my pillars crumbled. I stood on shaky ground for a long time. It took years to recover my balance and strengthen the pillars that remained. And in that time, I transformed. So many aspects of my life changed that I can hardly imagine the *"other life"* I once lived.

As a holistic therapist, my beliefs were challenged. I had lost my identity- not just as a therapist, as a daughter, a sister, a wife, and a mother.

∞

Nine years after Dad and Susan gained their Angel Wings, I decided that I wanted to publish a book exploring how grief shapes us throughout our lives. The plan was to publish the book in August 2024, 10 years after Susan had gained her Angel Wings, and dedicate it to Dad and Susan.

After speaking with people, I realised that an anthology, written from the heart by those who had experienced grief in different ways and navigated their own unique journeys, could offer hope and the inspiration to others. My goal was to show that, no matter how painful the process, transformation is possible, and healing can come in time with understanding, a little help from your friends or other people, and awareness. I started contacting people in November 2023 and getting the project off the ground.

Life, however, had other plans.

I truly believed that I had already weathered the worst storms of my life, emerged stronger, and grasped what this so-called "grief process" was all about. Transformation, growth, expansion-part of life's journey, or so I thought. And it is. What I hadn't yet discovered was what lies at the very heart of grief-the *gift* it quietly carries. In 2024, that truth was about to be revealed to me.

My Mum had been in a slow decline since 2014, and last year, 2024, it felt as if she had lost her spirit. There were brief moments when she rallied, but they became increasingly rare.

On the 14th of September 2024, we had a special reason to celebrate; it was Mum's eldest sister, my aunt Anne's 90th birthday, followed by my sister Sandra's 60th birthday on the 15th of September. Our family never needs an excuse for a party and this was one we were *definitely* not going to miss.

Mum was lucky enough to have 4 great grandsons; Lucas, Evan, (Mini-)Peter, and Morgan. She had met Morgan, Lucas and Evan though she had still to meet Peter. She called him *her Spanish baby*, because he was the image of his beautiful Spanish mother, Maria. Mum was so excited that we were all going to be there for the party, and every time I called her, that was all she talked about.

Sandra kept me updated on how Mum was doing, although with each video call, I could see her decline. Often, she didn't answer when I called because she was asleep.

I wanted to fly over to be with Mum, to care for her, but she was adamant that I should not get on a plane. She kept insisting that I wait and fly over as planned for the party with Keri, Lucas, and Evan.

It was eating me up inside. I wanted to be there to support my sister and brother, to care for Mum, and I also wanted to respect her wishes. In one of our rare conversations about this, I had promised her that when the time came, I would not go against her wishes. I had also promised that I would be there to make sure she was not in pain or feeling scared- but how could I do that if I were in another country?

I also had a job and family here in Mallorca. My sister wanted me there even though she knew that they would need me later, and she wanted me to be able to stay when that moment arrived.

We were all struggling being apart, and no one truly knew what the *right* thing was.

My son, Peter (hence *Mini-Peter*, his son), asked me if I thought he should fly over with Mini or wait until they were all going for the party. I couldn't give him a simple answer, however, what I did say was that if he wanted to be sure that his Gran met his son, he should get on the first available flight, and he did, thankfully.

My suitcase sat by the door, packed for over a week. When he flew over, after speaking to him and seeing Mum on the video-call, I decided enough was enough; I had to go.

I was so glad I went. I arrived on the 30th of August. My daughter Niki, who lives in England, had driven up to meet me and pick me up at the airport. We were both working that day and we went straight to my sister's house to work. We hadn't told Mum that I was coming.

Later that afternoon, when I finished work, I went to Mum's. She didn't give me a hard time about coming over early. I knew deep down it was the right decision for me to be there. She didn't put up much of an argument against me staying with her either.

I had made the right choice.

We all spent as much time with Mum as we could over the next few days. She was determined that she was going to make the party. Her making it to the party wouldn't have surprised us.

She refused to sleep, only managing a few hours when she lay on the couch and really could not force herself up again. Somehow, her body just kept going. It was incredible to witness her sheer determination to survive.

I was exhausted and sleep wasn't an option until one of the family members came in during the day. Night after night, I lay on the couch watching her struggle to get up and down, refusing my help. No matter how much she struggled, she kept insisting, *"Go to your bed. I'm fine!"*

Mum gained her Angel Wings twelve days after I arrived at 07.30 on the 11th of September 2024. Sandra and I stayed with her through the night. I had promised her I would be with her, and I was. For that, I will always be thankful.

What I wasn't prepared for was the impact of losing Mum. She had been slowly declining for so long—losing weight over the years, her breathing becoming more laboured. She was a shadow of her former self. Yet nothing could have prepared me for the shock of looking at her that morning and knowing she had taken her last breath.

With Dad, and then Susan passing so quickly, I honestly thought nothing could be worse-but grief has no limits.

There are no words to describe it. Now, when others are grieving, I simply say, *"There are no words, I'm here if you need me."*

Mum's passing left me without a place in this world. I became a little lost girl without my Mum. I didn't know who I was; I felt an overwhelming insecurity, a deep sense of not belonging. *Who was I?* My foundation had been shaken to its core. I didn't think my heart could take any more; it was in pieces again, and I didn't know how I was ever going to put it back together. Even now, I can't say it's fully whole. What I can tell you is, with the love and support of my family and friends, I am discovering who I am, again, piece by piece.

Now it's clear to me that the most challenging aspect of grief is the loss of identity.

We experience grief again and again, and each time, we emerge transformed. This is the process by which we grow and mature throughout life. However, that transformation is not always complete – sometimes we struggle to find the *gift* hidden within the pain. The "*new*" version of ourselves. Who we have become-our new identity.

I now believe that grief isn't something you simply "get over" or "move on" from—it's an experience that shapes you. It weaves itself into the fabric of your life, not as a wound that never heals, but as a force that transforms you. Grief invites you to grow, to deepen your understanding of love and loss, and to find meaning in the midst of sorrow. If you can uncover the gift hidden within grief, it no longer feels like something to escape, rather it becomes a profound part of your journey—one that reshapes your perspective and allows you to carry both loss and love forward in a new way.

Grief is a journey, not a destination. We are not meant to remain there.

When you lose someone you love- whether through death, separation, or your Munchkins flying the nest- the greatest loss is not just **them**, it is who **you** were to them.

When you retire, you lose a part of your work identity. For some, a career has been a constant throughout their adult life—shaping their purpose, routine, and sense of self. And then, suddenly, it's gone. The loss can feel profound, leaving them wondering, *Who am I without my job?*

There are countless moments in life when we experience grief—a loss of identity that comes with change. Grief isn't just about death; it can follow divorce, illness, retirement, or any major life transition. Many people feel lost, depressed, or disconnected, often without understanding why.

After all, isn't retirement meant to bring freedom? Watching your children grow up and move out—shouldn't that be a joyful milestone?

And just the same, these moments can carry an unexpected sense of loss.

So why do so many of us feel the opposite of what we are "supposed" to feel?

Because we no longer recognise ourselves. We feel as though we've lost a part of our identity.

And with identity comes purpose—a reason for being.

Isn't that what it's all about?

This is the *gift* you discover when you truly move *through* the grieving process.

You may feel that you've lost a part of yourself—you haven't. You can never lose who you were; you can only transform into more. You **BE***come* because of the person or thing that is now physically gone.

You still carry everything they meant to you, everything they taught you, and all the love you still hold for them. It remains within.

Nothing and no one can ever take that away from you—except ***you***.

Honour the people and experiences that have shaped your life. Welcome them. Appreciate them. All of them. Do not dishonour them by refusing to grow and **BE***come.*

Like a caterpillar in its chrysalis, take the time you need to move through grief in your own unique way. Allow transformation to happen. And when you are ready, emerge—renewed, strengthened, and prepared to embrace the next cycle of your life.

The gift is YOU.

Navigating Grief

Gentle Reminders When You're Hurting

These are some tips that may help you navigate your way through the grief process.

There's no right or wrong way—only what works for you.

Let it out.

That might mean talking with others, crying, ranting, joining a group, or attending therapy.

Try different things—you might feel lighter for it.

It's okay to ask for support.

And it's just as okay if you're not ready to ask. If you can, let people know what you need. That might change from day to day, and that's okay too.

Be kind to yourself.

Grief is exhausting—physically, emotionally, mentally.

Rest when you need to.

Eat when you can.

Try not to judge yourself for how you're coping.

There's no 'should' in grief.

Feel what you feel.

There may be moments of anger, guilt, numbness, laughter, even joy—and that's all part of it.

Nothing is wrong with you. You're human, and your grief is yours alone.

Stay connected.

Whether it's family, friends, a pet, a favourite place, or even a routine—small connections can help you feel grounded.

You don't have to go through it all alone.

Grief comes in waves.

Some days will feel manageable. Others might knock you off your feet.

Neither means you're going backwards.

Let the waves come—ride them however you can.

Breathe. You've survived every one so far.

You don't have to have it all together.

Even if people expect you to be "strong" or "getting on with things," remember—you're allowed to fall apart. You're allowed to feel lost.

You're allowed to not know what you need.

You are allowed!

Routines can help.

Simple things like getting out of bed, making a cup of tea, or going for a short walk can offer a bit of structure when everything feels chaotic.

Start small—one step at a time.

Memory and meaning matter.

It's okay to laugh. It's okay to remember.

To talk about the person you've lost.

To keep something of theirs close.

To create something new in their honour.

Grief is love, still finding its way.

And grief doesn't only come with death.

You might be grieving the loss of a job, a relationship, your health, or a version of life you imagined.

You might be adjusting to children leaving home or facing a change that reshapes who you are.

Whatever the loss, it's valid.

You're allowed to feel it deeply.

You're allowed to miss what was.

You're allowed to take time to figure out what comes next.

You are allowed!

Even in these moments, memory and meaning matter.

You can carry forward what was good, honour what has changed, and still find hope in what's to come.

And finally—go gently.

Wherever you are in your grief, you are doing your best.

Some days will look like surviving, and some days will look like healing.

Both are enough.

You are not alone.

> ***With love, from someone who's been there.***

Experience

Ralph Waldo Emerson

The lords of life, the lords of life—

    I saw them pass,

In their own guise,

Like and unlike,

Portly and grim,

Use and Surprise,

Surface and Dream,

Succession swift, and spectral Wrong,

Temperament without a tongue,

And the inventor of the game

Omnipresent without name; —

Some to see, some to be guessed,

They marched from east to west:

Little man, least of all,

Among the legs of his guardians tall,

Walked about with puzzled look: —

Him by the hand dear nature took;

Dearest nature, strong and kind,

Whispered, 'Darling, never mind!

Tomorrow they will wear another face,

The founder thou! these are thy race!'

from Essays: Second series (1844)

Ralph Waldo Emerson wrote "Experience" (1844) after the death of his young son, a major schism in his life, and yet the essay is notable for the fact that Emerson pointedly refuses to demonstrate his grief. You can download the full essay at https://emersoncentral.com/texts/essays-second-series/experience/

About the Authors

Anon

Linda Ledwidge

Gail Ledwidge   Jenny Ledwidge

Sue Berry   Lisa Ferris   Glynis German

Stephanie Schulz   Vicki McLeod   Deirdre Maguire

Ayelet Baron   Laura Penn

Amanda J Butler

Valou

ANTHOLOGY

"People are like diamonds—formed under pressure, shaped by time, and shining not despite their flaws, but because of them."

Glynis German

Growing Through Tears

Independent celebrant / End-of-life doula / Funeral planner / Death Cafe™ facilitator / Founder of the Giving Life to Death Festival.

B orn in Jamaica to a Jamaican mother and a Welsh father, moving to the UK as a young child and then travelling the world before settling in Spain at the end of her 20s has left its mark. Glynis enjoys being the outsider looking in, and she loves to tell stories. Whether it be a story that begins at the start of life, in the middle, or even at the end, Glynis tries to include the essence of the hero or heroine of her stories by focusing on their true qualities.

ANTHOLOGY

Student and apprentice mother to two beautiful sons, so obviously sent to teach her to let go and to grow, she lives in Mallorca in a small town whose Arab name means children of peace. Using universal, spiritual values as tools in which to support others, Glynis' goal in life is to be of use and to eventually die healthily, happily, and consciously alive right up until the end.

Contact details:

Email: glynis@glynisgermanfunerals.com

Website: https://glynisgermanfunerals.com

Facebook: https://www.facebook.com/GlynisGermanFunerals

Instagram: @glynisgermanfunerals

GROWING THROUGH GRIEF

Stephanie Schulz

Empty Nest

Radio Presenter | Author | Podcaster | Moderator | Public Speaker | Happy Human

Born in Düsseldorf, Germany, Stephanie Schulz is a seasoned radio presenter and author with a deep passion for exploring the souls of people and places. Her rich understanding of sociocultural diversity stems from years of living in Argentina, Brazil, Switzerland, and Costa Rica, as well as extensive travels—until she ultimately found her heart's home in Mallorca.

ANTHOLOGY

Stephanie is the co-author of *Faces of Mallorca*, an interview and photography book that captures the island's vibrant personalities and has been translated into multiple languages. She shares her storytelling talent with international audiences through compelling interviews, event moderation, and contributions to renowned publications.

Contact details:

Email: steffi@thecreativefactory.org

Website: www.thecreativefactory.org

Instagram: @steph.writes

GROWING THROUGH GRIEF

Gail Ledwidge

GRIEF, grief, GRIEF

Mother / Wife / Sister / Best friend

Gail is someone who cares deeply and shares generously with the world.

Multi-talented yet profoundly humble, she approaches life with a big heart, always offering kindness, wisdom, and unwavering support to those around her.

ANTHOLOGY

"Those who've known grief shine differently—like diamonds formed in the deep, their light carries a strength only time and love can create."

Jenny Ledwidge

Growing Through the Love

Registered Children's and Young People's Nurse / Trained low-intensity Cognitive Behavioural Therapy (CBT) practitioner

Born in Birmingham to Northern Irish parents, Joan and Gerry, the youngest of four children—Ray, Clare, Maria, and Jenny. They were raised by their Mom, Joan, who continues to inspire Jenny every day, even after her passing. Jenny's deep connection to her Irish heritage shapes her values and approach to life. Her personal experience with grief has fuelled her passion for supporting others in their mental health journeys.

ANTHOLOGY

Contact details:

Facebook: https://www.facebook.com/JenLedwidge

Instagram: @jenledwidge

LinkedIn: Jenny Ledwidge

GROWING THROUGH GRIEF

Laura Penn

Grief is Tough

Media Professional / Presenter / Author

Seasoned media professional with a strong background in creating compelling written, audio, and visual content.

Beyond content creation, Laura has a wealth of experience in management and radio airtime sales, having worked across the UK and Spain. Her diverse skill set and deep understanding of the media landscape make her a valuable asset in both creative and commercial aspects of the industry.

In addition to her work in broadcasting, Laura is also a published author, further showcasing her talent for storytelling and communication.

ANTHOLOGY

"Grief changes people. It puts them under pressure, in the dark, and over time, something stronger, clearer, and more resilient takes shape—like a diamond born of everything it endured."

GROWING THROUGH GRIEF

Valou

Grief is the Process by which We Manage to Live Serenely with the Loss of Someone or Something

Emotional Wellness Coach & Personal Development Advocate

Mother to Luna (22) and Sasha (18), Valou discovered Faster EFT (Eutaptics) over 12 years ago during a difficult separation. Initially drawn to the technique as a way to help her children navigate their emotions, she soon realised it was the catalyst for her profound journey of introspection, self-awareness, and emotional transformation.

ANTHOLOGY

Through her practice, Valou developed a deep trust in life's unfolding, embracing challenges as lessons for growth and opportunities to become the best version of oneself. With this philosophy, she reframes negative experiences into positive perspectives, embodying a mindset of resilience and flow.

Believing in the power of self-development and emotional well-being, Valou inspires others to embrace life as it comes—trusting that when we let go, the rest will follow.

Contact details:

Email: freebytapping@hotmail.com

GROWING THROUGH GRIEF

Deirdre Maguire

Transforming Grief into Hope

Mind Wellness Specialist / Speaker / Author / Creator of The Stress Solution System

With a passion for helping people break free from limiting thought patterns, Deirdre empowers individuals worldwide to achieve happiness and fulfilment. Her journey into this work began after her father's tragic suicide and deepened when Deirdre faced her own cancer diagnosis, driving her to develop powerful life management skills.

ANTHOLOGY

Deirdre's personal experiences have shaped her professional mission—to ensure no one feels as lost as she once did. Today, she shares transformative tools to help others embrace joy and live fully.

Contact details:

Email: freedom@deirdremaguire.com

Website: www.deirdremaguire.com

Facebook: https://www.facebook.com/wisdomofireland

YouTube: www.youtube.com/wisdomofireland

Instagram: https://www.instagram.com/deirdre.maguire

GROWING THROUGH GRIEF

Lisa Ferris

Grief

Lisa Ferris is a strong, independent woman with a big, loving heart.

For the past 20 years, she has been on a journey to find a place she can truly call home—a space where she feels secure and cherished. Now, Lisa is embracing the beauty of her life and, most importantly, learning to love herself. Her story is one of resilience, self-discovery, and the pursuit of inner peace.

ANTHOLOGY

"Grief carves us like the slow hand of the earth forming a diamond—pressed by memory, shaped by loss, and polished by love. What remains is not what we were, but something quietly radiant."

Ayelet Baron

Grief Reveals Us

Visionary thinker / Award-winning author who left the fast-paced world of Silicon Valley to explore the depths of human potential / Recognised as one of the top female futurists

Ayelet has dedicated herself to reminding us of our innate power as creators. Her journey has been one of continuous transformation, likening her experiences to "dying many times" as she learns and experiments in uncharted territories. Her literary work spans both the professional and personal realms, with four acclaimed books on conscious business and a thought-provoking trilogy on life itself. Ayelet's writing reflects her belief that humanity stands at a pivotal moment in history, one where each individual has the capacity to shape the future. Through her work, Ayelet encourages us to view challenges as opportunities and to embrace the unknown with curiosity and courage. Her approach combines practical insights from her corporate background with a deep understanding of human nature, offering a unique perspective on navigating our rapidly changing world.

Contact details:

Website: https://ayeletbaron.com

Twitter/X: https://x.com/ayeletb/

Instagram: https://www.instagram.com/ayeletb/

LinkedIn: https://www.linkedin.com/ayeletbaron/

GROWING THROUGH GRIEF

Amanda J. Butler

Grief and Loss

Conscious entrepreneur / Adventurer / Seeker / Wellness Warrior

Spiritual but not religious (SBNR), Amanda embraces life with a carpe diem mindset, believing that "all my experiences = the sum of my parts."

Inspired by her mother's passing from cancer, Amanda is passionate about making wellness and holistic therapies more accessible worldwide. She is the co-founder of Wellness Traveller, a conscious travel company dedicated to integrating wellness into travel experiences.

In addition, Amanda offers her expertise as a holistic buyer's agent, specialising in wellness real estate in Mallorca, and shares her insights through a wellness column in the Majorca Daily Bulletin and Celebrity Magazine in Mallorca.

ANTHOLOGY

Contact details:

Email: amanda@wellnesstraveller.co

Website: https://wellnesstraveller.co

Facebook: https://www.facebook.com/wellnesstraveller.co

Instagram: https://www.instagram.com/wellnesstraveller.co/

GROWING THROUGH GRIEF

Vicki McLeod

Signs of Life

Writer / Journalist / Photographer

Vicki is a writer, journalist, and photographer with extensive experience in print and digital media. She has written for newspapers and magazines in both the UK and Spain, covering a wide range of topics, including Spanish culture, entrepreneurship, business, travel, and human interest stories. She specialises in interview-based features that bring out the depth and nuance of her subjects.

As the founder of Phoenix Media Mallorca, Vicki provides editorial and content marketing services to businesses, helping them communicate clearly and impactfully. Her work spans long-form journalism, editorial

ANTHOLOGY

features, and brand storytelling, always with a focus on precision, authenticity, and narrative strength. Alongside her writing, she is also a photographer with a particular interest in capturing portraits that reflect character and emotion. She is the co-founder of Mariposa Photography, a new collaboration dedicated to photographing women with honesty and artistry.

Committed to fostering a creative writing community, Vicki has recently launched The Teapot Writing Room, a space for writers to gather, focus, and develop their work in a supportive environment.

Based in Mallorca, she continues to contribute to publications while working with businesses and individuals to craft engaging, high-quality content.

Contact details:

Email: phoenixmediamallorca@gmail.com

Website: https://www.phoenix-media-mallorca.com

Facebook: https://www.facebook.com/PhoenixMediaMallorca

Instagram: https://www.instagram.com/phoenixmediamallorca/

GROWING THROUGH GRIEF

Linda Ledwidge

Life Goes On

Mum / Nini / Inspirer of JOY / Author / Human BEing

Linda Ledwidge is dedicated to empowering individuals to lead healthier, happier lives by discovering what uniquely works for them. Originally from Glasgow and raised in East Kilbride, she has called Mallorca home since 1996.

Her healthcare journey began in the 1980s when she trained as a General Nurse and Midwife in Glasgow. With a deep curiosity about the mind-body connection and a passion for healing, she has continuously expanded her expertise across various therapeutic modalities.

Today, her mission is simple yet powerful: **to change the world, one person at a time**—helping others find the tools and knowledge they need to cultivate a healthy body and a joyful life.

ANTHOLOGY

This book was born from Linda's belief that she had weathered life's storms and finally understood what this thing called "grief" was all about. Just as she began bringing the project to life, however, the universe threw her another curveball—reminding her there was still more to learn.

Amid the twists and turns, Linda has come to appreciate that she may *never* fully figure it out—and that perhaps she's not meant to. She believes that we are all on a continuous journey of growth, expansion, and transformation. Each time we move through this cycle, we experience something we call "*grief*."

Linda also believes that within every cycle of grief lies a hidden *gift*. Our mission is to find the *gift*—because it's in that discovery that we truly grow, expand, and transform. Or, as Linda likes to say—**BE**come.

Through her writing, Linda shares her wisdom, guiding and inspiring others on their own paths to well-being and true **JOY**.

Contact details:

Email: linda@lindaledwidge.com

Website: https://www.lindaledwidge.com

Instagram: https://www.instagram.com/lindalive2017/

LinkedIn: https://www.linkedin.com/in/lindaanneledwidge/

YouTube: https://www.youtube.com/@LindaLedwidge9166

Grief resources

DESIGNED FOR WHEN YOU OR SOMEONE YOU CARE ABOUT NEEDS SUPPORT IN NAVIGATING LOSS

This is a list of grief resources designed for when you or someone you care about needs support in navigating loss. It includes a variety of helplines, websites and communities covering different types of grief such as bereavement, anticipatory grief, and non-death losses.

Support Lines (UK-based)

- **Cruse Bereavement Support** | Helpline: 0808 808 1677

Free, confidential support for anyone grieving. Offers online chats, local services, and a national helpline.

- **The Good Grief Trust** thegoodgrieftrust.org

A hub of UK-based grief support organisations and services, tailored by type of loss.

- **Child Bereavement UK** childbereavementuk.org | Helpline: 0800 02 888 40

Support for families when a child dies or is facing death, and for children grieving the loss of someone close.

- **Samaritans** samaritans.org | Call: 116 123 (free, 24/7)

For anyone feeling overwhelmed or struggling to cope—grief included.

Online Communities & Resources

- **What's Your Grief**

Articles, podcasts, courses, and a blog covering every corner of grief—from the practical to the deeply personal.

- **Let's Talk About Loss** letstalkaboutloss.org

A peer support group for young people aged 18–35 who are grieving.

- **Grief Encounter** griefencounter.org.uk

Tailored support for bereaved children and young people, with resources for schools and families too.

Creative & Reflective Tools

- **Grief journals**

- **Memory boxes** – collecting photos, letters, small keepsakes.

- **Therapeutic art or collage** – can be incredibly expressive, even with no words.

- **Rituals or ceremonies** – lighting a candle, planting a tree, writing letters.

1. Grief from Job Loss

- **Career Transition Resources**

  - *CareerOneStop* (U.S.) – Tools for job search, career transitions, and coping with unemployment.

- **Online Communities**

  - *Workplace Grief Forum* – Many grief support forums now have sections for job loss. https://forums.grieving.com/

2. Grief from Illness (Chronic or Terminal)

- **Support Lines and Organizations**

  - *Macmillan Cancer Support* (UK) – macmillan.org.uk | Helpline: 0808 808 00 00

Offers emotional and practical support for those living with cancer and their families.

- *CancerCare* (U.S.) – cancercare.org | Helpline: 800-813-HOPE (4673)

Counseling and support services for cancer patients and families.

- **Online Communities**

  - *HealthUnlocked* – healthunlocked.com

A network of patient support communities for chronic illnesses and long-term health conditions.

- *CaringBridge* – caringbridge.org

A platform to create personal websites for loved ones facing illness, allowing for community updates and support.

3. Grief from Loss of a Parent

- **Support Lines and Organizations**
  - *The Compassionate Friends* (U.S. & UK) – compassionatefriends.org

Provides support for parents grieving the loss of a child, but also has sections for those dealing with the loss of a parent.

- *Grief Recovery Institute* – griefrecoverymethod.com

Offers resources for any type of loss, including loss of a parent, with a structured recovery method.

- **Online Communities**
  - *The Bereavement Network* – bereavement.co.uk

A UK-based resource that connects people grieving the loss of a parent to online support groups.

- *GriefSupport.com* – griefsupport.com

A global platform offering grief support groups for a variety of losses, including the death of a parent.

4. Grief from Loss of a Relationship

- **Support Lines and Organizations**

  ○ *Relate* (UK) – relate.org.uk | Call: 0300 100 1234

Relationship counseling services for individuals and couples.

- *DivorceCare* (U.S.) – divorcecare.org

Support for people navigating the grief of divorce, separation, or breakup, including group meetings and resources.

- **Online Communities**

  ○ *Reddit's r/BreakUps* – reddit.com/r/breakups

A community focused on support and advice for individuals going through the end of a relationship.

"Even in the darkness of grief, love still flickers—quiet, but never gone."

Afterword

This project has been one of the most challenging, emotional, and fulfilling undertakings of my life, and I deeply appreciate the courage it took for each and every author to open their hearts.

Thank you all for trusting me with your innermost thoughts and feelings.

I am incredibly proud of everyone who has contributed to this book, and I know that sharing their experiences will offer support and comfort to people all over the world.

My hope is that each person who reads this book will pass it on—to a family member, a friend, or a support group that may benefit from it.

Linda xc

You Got This.
free flo living
www.lindaledwidge.com

ANTHOLOGY

"Souls touched by grief are like divine diamonds—formed in unseen depths, refined through pain, and destined to reflect a light not of this world, but of love eternal."

Notes

"Grief is the price of having something so beautiful, even goodbye couldn't take it away."

ANTHOLOGY

GROWING THROUGH GRIEF

ANTHOLOGY

GROWING THROUGH GRIEF

ANTHOLOGY

"Grief rewrites you. You'll never be the same story, but you're still worth reading."

Made in the USA
Las Vegas, NV
01 May 2025